Selections from the poetry of Baššār

edited with translation and commentary
and an Introductory Sketch of Arabic poetic structures by

A.F.L.BEESTON

Cambridge University Press
Cambridge
London · New York · Melbourne

Published by the Syndics of the Cambridge University Press
The Pitt Building, Trumpington Street, Cambridge CB2 1RP
Bentley House, Euston Road, London NW1 2DB
32 East 57th Street, New York, NY 10022, U.S.A.
296 Beaconsfield Parade, Middle Park, Melbourne 3206, Australia

First published 1977

Printed in Great Britain at the University Press, Cambridge

Library of Congress Cataloguing in Publication Data

Bashshār ibn Burd, d. 783 or 4
Selections from the poetry of Baššār
Text in English and Arabic
Bibliography: p.

I. Beeston, Alfred Felix Landon II. Title
PJ7741.B3A6 1977 892'.7'132 77-928
ISBN 0 521 21664 8 hard covers
ISBN 0 521 29223 9 paperback

Selections from the poetry of Baššār

CONTENTS

INTRODUCTION

AIM. The aim of this work is to provide students of Arabic in their second year with a first introduction to classical Arabic poetry; it being assumed that they will by then have gained sufficient acquaintance with the language to read Standard Prose with reasonable ease. It is also assumed that in the course of their first year they will have become familiar with basic technicalities like *hamzat al-waṣl, ḥāl, &c*.

The blind poet Baššār b. Burd seems to me particularly suitable for this purpose. His amatory pieces are drafted in relatively simple language, and present very few vocabulary difficulties; and they are more congruous with Western taste than most other classical Arabic poetry. From these, one can proceed through specimens of other genres to that of Eulogy, which is (at least to start with) the most difficult for a European reader to appreciate.

For the life of the poet, the reader is advised to consult the second edition of the *Encyclopaedia of Islam*.

BACKGROUND. The poet's lifetime (c.96 - 167 A.H.) straddles a major watershed in Arabic literature: the transition from the Umayyad to the Abbasid age.

Pre-Islamic poetry had been above all a poetry of the desert, deeply stamped with characteristics imposed on it by the special conditions of the bedouin life. By reason of the tribal structure of bedouin society, it is a poetry in which the poet's individuality is in many cases blurred by the overpowering pressure of non-individualistic tribal solidarity feelings; as a result, the poetry tends to be outward-looking and objective, rather than subjective and introspective. Its appeal to the feelings of the audience was made through sensuous images, rather than by way of the intellect. Above all, it uses an immense vocabulary. In part, this is simply due to the bedouin environment: vast areas of human thought and experience simply did not exist for the bedouin with their narrow and specialized desert life-style, but in compensation for this the bedouin had an extremely detailed vocabulary for every aspect of life as it did present itself to them in the limited field of their experience. An enormous number of terms, including those for every detail connected with camels, horses, and the fauna, flora and other phenomena of the desert, are to us - and indeed to the Arabs of later times - strange and difficult words (*ḡarā'ib*), whereas to the bedouin they were the normal currency of everyday life. One could compare their outlook with that of a sailor, to whom the immense technical vocabulary of ships is an everyday familiarity, whereas to the landsman these terms are strange and unfamiliar *ḡarā'ib*. Add to this a large stock of synonyms for even the simplest and most basic concepts, which is probably to be accounted for by the fusion of various dialects in the poetic 'common tongue'. Finally, there is little doubt that the early poets (and their audiences) took a delight in genuinely unusual words for their own sake. This has been a commonplace of poetic diction in all ages, for with a few exceptions (such as Thomas Gray, William Cowper and William Wordsworth) poets have felt that poetry demands a language uncontaminated by the banalities of everyday intercourse; even Aeschylus had fun poked at him by Aristophanes on this score, and although over-indulgence can lead to the disasters of the 'Wardour Street style' (and its 'bosky groves' &c), most of the great poets have on the whole avoided commonplace language.

The advent of Islam at first did little to change the situation of poetry, since early Muslim poets were still Arabs working within a tradition which had already established conventions and rules. The effect of Islam was mainly the external one, that the more puritanical Muslims disapproved of poetry altogether: partly because the conventional modes were deeply imprinted with the bedouin outlook and ethics, which Muslims felt had been done away with by Islam, and belonged to a barbaric past (*jāhiliyyah*); also perhaps because of Quranic remarks in condemnation of poets. It must however be remarked that these belong to the Meccan period of revelation, and relate to a situation in which, being exposed to the satirical attacks of pagan Qurayš poets, the Muslims had no means of retaliation; yet in the Medinan period, the Prophet himself showed no reluctance to accept the services of Anṣārī poets. Ḥassān b.Ṯābit became virtually court poet, and Kaᶜb b.Zuhayr's most famous poem is in praise of the Prophet; these poems were cast in the traditional moulds, and Kaᶜb's poem praises the Prophet in the same style as his father had used before Islam for praising tribal chieftains.

It was not to be expected that the Arab aristocracy of the Umayyad period should welcome any change in the poetic climate. Charles Pellat has remarked (*Langue et littérature arabes*, Paris 1952, p.78):

> The prime reason for this survival is that the Arabs who had established themselves in the conquered countries were bedouin, attached to their old habits and animated by a desire to re-evoke their deserts, if only in their poetry. Moreover, the Umayyad caliphs and high officials of the administration were Arabs: thus they strove to promote an Arab policy, and gave a favourable welcome to any bedouin who resorted to them. When they themselves were not poets, they retained a special taste for bedouin poetry.

The poets of the latter half of the first century of Islam were hence basically bedouin poets of the ancient stamp. Yet already a note of artificiality was creeping in. The inescapable fact was that, however much the Umayyad princes in their desert hunting lodges might like to fancy themselves as Arab chieftains of the ancient pattern, the bulk of even the pure Arab population of the Islamic realm was abandoning the desert environment and settling down to an urbanized or at least sedentarized life. On top of this, vast crowds of non-Arab clients were flocking into Islam and building up a culture which, though Arabic speaking, was only to a limited extent Arab in outlook.

As soon, therefore, as the political power of the Umayyads began to totter, these new forces began to make themselves felt in poetry, generating a 'modernistic' school with an outlook greatly at variance with that prevailing before. Baššār was in the forefront of this movement. Yet even so, there is a fundamental dichotomy in his work. In parts, specially in his amatory pieces, we see a bold seeking out of new ways, characterized by an economy of vocabulary and by an intensity of personal feeling alien to the bedouin style, and comparable with the reaction of Cowper and Wordsworth against the increasingly stilted Augustanism of much eighteenth century verse. This brought Baššār great popularity, specially among the younger generation, but it did not gain him a livelihood. For his bread and butter he depended, as a professional poet, on the composition of eulogistic pieces in praise of patrons able to reward him for them. These patrons wished to be celebrated in traditional style, and would not have welcomed or rewarded over-bold excursions into the 'modernistic' idiom. The poet himself does not seem to have felt this obligation burdensome, for he manifestly took a pride in being able to compose successfully in both the new and the traditional style. There is one piece, beginning *Bakkirā ṣāhibayya*, which he is said explicitly to have composed in order to display his skill in manipulating the ancient style and his familiarity with its *ġarā'ib*. But pieces of this kind are literary tours-de-force, with an artificiality far removed from the directness of feeling expressed in the amatory poems. When this blind poet of Basra depicts scenes of desert life, which he cannot have experienced at first hand, he was displaying his skill in copying the old masters. The European reader desirous of becoming acquainted with the glories of bedouin poetry will probably prefer to tackle the older poets themselves. Baššār's descriptive pieces are therefore not included in this selection, except insofar as they may be too intimately integrated into a eulogistic poem to be sidetracked.

The best Arabic poetry is immensely musical, and until one has attuned one's ear to its rhythms and music, the task of elucidating the meaning of the ancient bedouin poets can be a dry and heartbreaking one. It is my hope that an initial approach by way of Baššār may help towards acquiring such an appreciation. Yet even his modernistic pieces are not without their own problems: they are highly allusive, in a way that bedouin poetry is usually not, and they often presuppose a familiarity with earlier tradition, one word serving to evoke a range of images with which it had become associated in the ancient style. The remarks which follow on Poetic Conventions aim at outlining some of the commonest features which must be borne in mind in this connection.

The early Abbasid urbanized language is the foundation of modern Standard Arabic, and it is noticeable that, with a very few exceptions, Wehr's *Dictionary of Modern Written Arabic* contains all the vocabulary needed for reading Baššār's modernistic pieces. But as the student progresses through the sections of this selection, he will probably find himself increasingly driven to supplement this by recourse to the great dictionary of Lane. The commentaries, however, deal with some of the trickier vocabulary points.

THE TEXTUAL SOURCES. There are three principal primary sources:

1. As is the case with all early Arabic poetry, an important source is Abū l-Faraj al-Iṣfahānī's *Kitāb al-Ag̅ānī*; this contains a long section devoted to our poet, as well as some quotations elsewhere in the book, amounting in all to approximately 600 lines of his poetry. This is cited here by the page numbers of the Cairo *Dār al-kutub* edition (vol.3, 1929), with the siglum A.

2. An ancient copy (attributed to the latter sixth century A.H.) of the first half of Baššār's *Dīwān* or collected poems - comprising the rhymes from *alif* to *r* - is extant in the Zaytūna mosque in Tunis. This has a commentary by the modern Tunisian scholar Muḥammad al-Ṭāhir Ibn ᶜĀšūr; and the text and commentary were published by Muḥammad Rifᶜat Fatḥ Allah and Muḥammad Šawqī Amīn, together with additional notes by those editors, in three volumes (Cairo, 1950). This is cited here by volume and page number with the siglum D.

3. An early anthology, *al-Muk̲tār min šiᶜr Baššār*, was compiled by two scholars of the fourth century A.H., Saᶜīd b.Hišām al-K̲ālidī and his brother Muḥammad; this was provided with a commentary by a fifth century scholar, Abū l-Ṭāhir Ismāᶜīl b.Aḥmad al-Tujībī. Like most Arabic anthologies, it is not a collection of complete poems, but of selected passages, generally fairly short. This is preserved in a manuscript in Haidarabad, and was first published by Muḥammad Badr al-Din al-ᶜAlawī at Aligarh (1935). A new edition of this appeared in Beirut from the *Dār al-t̲aqāfah* press in 1963; very confusingly, this new edition bears the title *Dīwān*, although it is in no sense a complete *dīwān*, but the Haidarabad *Muk̲tār*. This is cited here according to the numeration of the extracts, with the siglum M.

Two other, secondary, sources have been used. Some fifteen or so years ago, the Cairo *Dār al-Maᶜārif* press series *Nawābig̅ al-fikr al-ᶜarabī* issued (undated) a selection from Baššār made by Ṭāhā al-Ḥājirī for modern readers; a re-issue of it appeared in 1963, but with a different pagination from the original; this I have cited by page numbers of both issues, distinguishing them as H^1 and H^2. As a selection, this anthology has great attractions, presenting an excellent picture of the poet's work; and I have consequently taken it as the basis of the selection here offered. However, I have omitted Ḥājirī's second and sixth sections, containing imitations of the bedouin style, for the reason mentioned above; and I have added some extra pieces which seem to me to contain features of interest.

Finally, André Roman has published, under the title *Baššār et son expérience courtoise* (*Dar el-Machriq*, Beyrouth 1972), the amatory poems addressed to ᶜAbdah together with a French translation. To this, where necessary, I have referred (by page numbers) as R.

A major problem confronting anyone who has to deal with early Arabic poetry is that of textual variants. The sophisticated techniques of Western textual criticism cannot be applied because we lack sufficient evidence; there are virtually never enough manuscripts extant for them to be grouped into 'manuscript families' and for us to be able to trace the genesis and progress of corruptions, and frequently we are dependent on two or three sources with no criteria by which to judge their relative value. Nor is textual variation necessarily due to 'corruption'; the poets themselves were undoubtedly responsible for some of it. In the case of, e.g. Shelley, we can by a careful analysis of his notebooks follow the stages through which he worked to produce the final published version of a poem; this is impossible in the case of an Arabic poet, and we are often confronted with variants - some or all of which may possibly have originated with the author himself - but have no means of establishing any priority among them. The editors of D and M of course record the two manuscripts on which they were respectively working, though in the case of D they quite often propose emendations. Among all this conflicting evidence, what Ḥājirī has done is to present an eclectic text that reflects his own judgment of the most effective reading; I have followed the same procedure, though without always coming to the same conclusion as he has (in particular, both issues contain misprints which needed correction). I have not, however, produced a 'critical' text with reference to all the variants: the source references will enable those who wish to do so, to pursue the textual problems further.

POETIC CONVENTIONS. There are certain types of expression which are commonplaces in all Arabic poetry, and immediately understandable in an Arabic context, but if translated literally into English are either unintelligible, or convey a different sense from what the author intended, unless the reader has been made previously familiar with them.

1. Words meaning "time", particularly *dahr* and *zamān*, as well as both *al-ayyām* and *al-layālī*, are frequently used to imply the vicissitudes of time, and generally speaking they correspond to what an English writer would express by "Fortune" or "Fate".

2. In eulogy, all words associated with the idea of moisture (dew, rain, water, sea, ocean, clouds) imply generosity and bountifulness; and a great variety of metaphorical and figurative expressions are woven round this concept. Thunder and lightning, which portend rain, may also be used in the same way; but sometimes the thundercloud fails to produce the hoped-for rain, and it is then "deceitful" (*k̲ullab*) and may be applied to one who disappoints the expectations of suitors.

3. In descriptive passages, moisture implies youth, freshness and full flesh. Conversely, all words conveying the idea of dryness imply that which is lean, skinny and fleshless, whether by reason of age or of hardship and exertion.

4. In amatory passages, the Arab poet will sometimes speak of the lips and smile of his beloved, but rather more commonly he speaks of the saliva (*rīq*) where an English poet would talk of lips; and of teeth where the English one would talk of the smile. The teeth are usually referred to in poetry by the words *t̲anāyā* (strictly, "front teeth") or *t̲aḡr* (the teeth considered as the barrier or frontier of the mouth). Much imagery is built round these ideas.

5. Any emotion which causes the heart to pound (love, terror &c.) is compared to a 'bird in the breast' (not unlike the English locution of 'butterflies in the stomach').

6. Several conventional and recognised metaphors for war often form the basis of an allusion: war is a flame, which burns up the warring peoples; or a millstone (*raḥā*) which grinds them to powder; or a poisonous pool, from which anyone who drinks perishes.

7. More generally, heat of any kind connotes pain and anguish; conversely, coolness or shade connote tranquillity and comfort. With the Iraqi poets,

even "ice" can bear this meaning; though for the bedouin of the high plateau, winter cold was a feared thing.
8. In eulogy, references to journeying allude to the generosity of the patron; behind them lies the idea that the magnanimity of the patron is such that men will travel vast distances and overcome great obstacles in order to reach him.
9. One of the earliest surviving poems, the *Mu^{c}allaqah* of Umru' al-Qays, begins "Stop, my two friends!", although the two friends are shadowy and unidentified figures who play no further part in the poem. This habit of addressing a shadowy audience of two survived as a poetic convention long into the Abbasid age.
10. In amatory poetry, stock figures who are often accorded unfavourable mention are,

(a) the "reproacher" (*^{c}ātibah*, usually feminine), who criticizes the poet for his passion;

(b) the "watcher" (*raqīb*), whose jealous eye is always on the girl and prevents the lover from being alone with her;

(c) the "vilifier" (*wāšī* or *nāmī*), the tittle-tattle who publicizes the love-affair and makes it a theme of scandalous gossip.

11. The word *fatā*, which properly means a man in the prime of life (any time between his ceasing to be an adolescent, *ḡulām*, and around the age of forty when he becomes *šayk͟*), is frequently used in verse without any marked age reference, but simply as a synonym of *mar'* "man (in general)"; *rajul* is comparatively rare in verse.
12. A certain number of ancient bedouin expressions have become established in Abbasid language as clichés. One of the most noticeable of these is the formula of saying that something is *lillāhi* "pertaining to the deity". This stems ultimately from a very primitive feeling that anything out of the ordinary (whether admirable or terrible) has something supernatural and superhuman about it; but in Abbasid usage the phrase has been drained of its original force and has become a conventional mode of expressing wonderment: "how strange, how marvellous, how dreadful is ...".

General throughout Arabic verse is the omission of a pronoun which English feeling would regard as necessary for the meaning: e.g. *al-ḥubb* may have to be understood as "my love" or "your love" and not as "love" in general. Also common is the replacement of a genitive by a periphrasis with *min* or *li*: *al-ḥubb minnī* "my love", *ḥubb li-salmā* "the love of Salmā". Prepositional expressions may be separated from, or precede, the noun they qualify.

Chnage of person (*iltifāt*) is not uncommon; the same person may be spoken of as "you" and "he" in two immediately successive lines. This can be confusing to a European reader unaccustomed to this freedom (note e.g. the last line of VII in this selection).

Amatory poets often use third-person masculine forms when a woman is in fact meant. The explanation of this phenomenon has puzzled many Western critics. My own view is that it has a purely linguistic origin, and derives from the well-known fact that the relative-demonstrative *man* uses masculine singular concords irrespective of what gender or number is actually envisaged. Hence *man aḥbabtu-hū* is "the person I love" irrespective of gender, and this and similar phrases may be followed by quite a long string of further masculine pronoun references. Ultimately, the versifier has come to feel himself free to use masculine forms whenever it suits him.

NOTE ON TRANSLATION. It is a well-known truism that translation of poetry from one language into another is almost impossible, specially when the two languages have widely differing cultural backgrounds. It has certainly not been my aim here to produce renderings such as would give the English reader who knows no Arabic some conception of the original; but rather to assist the student towards appreciating the Arabic original. For this purpose, I regard it as essential that the English rendering should be reasonably idiomatic; what is known as a 'literal translation' may occasionally be of help in pointing out the grammatical structure of the original, but beyond that it is more of a hindrance than a help. In some places, therefore, I have not hesitated to use a fairly free paraphrase. It is important that the reader should bear this in mind when using the translations.

In some cases, it is absolutely necessary, in order to achieve an intelligible rendering, to add words which are only implicit and not explicitly present in the Arabic. A broken underline has been used to mark these when there seems special need to call attention to them.

METRE. 'Verse' and 'poetry', though commonly conjoined, are not the same thing. Verse is a form of diction with a specifically definable rhythmic effect on the ear, poetry is created by the meaning of the words used; one may have poetic diction which is not verse, and verse diction which is prosaic and unpoetical. But until the modern period, the Arabs have always restricted the application of the term *ši^{c}r* to diction which conforms to recognised verse rhythms; there is some truly poetic diction in Arabic literature which is nevertheless not accounted *ši^{c}r* because not in the accepted verse rhythms.

The earliest known Arabic poetry has already a limited range of clearly marked rhythms, resulting from a long period of development about which we know nothing. These rhythms were used by the early poets instinctively and by ear; no attempt was made to analyse, describe and name them until the latter part of the second century A.H., when the grammarian al-K̲alīl b.Aḥmad devised a systematic account which has remained normative down to the present day. This system has been criticized in some of its details, but even the rather radical re-appraisal made by Kamāl Abū Deeb (*Fī l-binyati l-īqā^{c}iyyati lil-ši^{c}ri l-^{c}arabī*, Beirut 1974) accepts the main principles of K̲alīl's system as valid.

Ancient Arabic verse had only two forms for a poem: there is the *qiṭ^{c}ah* or 'piece' of indeterminate length; and the *qaṣīdah* or 'formal ode' of around twenty to a hundred 'lines' (as defined below), and showing certain structural conventions. Poems in strophic or stanzaic form, and pieces of verse running to hundreds of lines, do not occur before the fourth century A.H.

Verse rhythms in English are constituted by a patterned contrast between two types of syllable, the stressed and the unstressed. Syllabic contrast is equally fundamental to Arabic verse, but is of a different kind, arising out of the nature of the language itself. The high-prestige language (less so the modern colloquials) does not admit an utterance beginning with a vowel (either *hamz* or some other consonant must precede); nor one beginning with two consonants without intervening vowel; nor, within a stretch of connected discourse, a cluster of more than two consonants without intervening vowel. These features lead to a syllabic analysis in which there are basically only two types of syllable, namely CV (a one-consonant syllable, hereafter '1c') and CVC (a two consonant syllable, hereafter '2c'); and this syllabic contrast underlies the whole system of verse rhythms.

In principle, V in this kind of syllabic analysis is a 'short' vowel, such as is represented in Arabic script by a vowel-mark and not by a letter of the alphabet. What Europeans usually term a 'long' vowel is evaluated as a short vowel plus a 'letter of prolongation' - *alif*, *w* or *y*. Thus the word for "in" is a 2c syllable *fiy*, exactly like *kam*. In the prosodic analyses which I shall give later, *ī* and *ū* are noted as *iy* and *uw*; but since there is no comparable European notation for the *alif* of prolongation, I have preserved the convention that a 2c syllable should have three Latin letters in the transcription by using *aa* for *ā*.

The basic principle, however, creates practical tensions in two ways. Within the limits of a single word, a syllable CaaC has to be admitted in some cases where it is essential for the sense: *jad.da.tun* "grandmother" contrasts with *jaad.da.tun* "road". But for prosodic purposes the two are not differentiated, and both have to be analysed as 2c.1c.2c. Secondly, in connected discourse, *hamzat al-waṣl* creates tension when the preceding word ends with a letter of prolongation; this tension is normally resolved by eliminating the letter of prolongation (i.e. the feature of 'length'), so that "in the house" has to be analysed as *fil.bay.ti* (2c.2c.1c).

The following account of the various rhythms is a summary one, omitting a good deal that is not essential for an appreciation of them; a more extended account will be found in the *Encyclopaedia of Islam*, under the entry ᶜARŪḌ. The traditional system lists sixteen rhythms or 'metres'. Nine of these are represented in the present selection, and these nine are all that the ordinary student of Arabic is likely to encounter. Taking as a test sample one volume of the *Kitāb al-A̱gānī*, out of 436 quotations which it gives, three metres are not represented at all, and another four appear in a total of only 25 quotations. It would thus appear that a familiarity with the nine favourite metres should enable the student to handle 95 per cent of Arabic poetry. Each independent poem in traditional verse is always in the same metre throughout; metrical mixtures are found only in strophic verse and in some modern productions.

A fundamental feature of the various distinctive rhythms is the incidence at regular intervals of a dissylabic 'nucleus' (traditionally called a "peg", *watid*, pl. *awtād*) consisting of two syllables of contrasting types, usually CV.CVC (1c.2c); K̲alīl did envisage the alternative possibility of a nucleus in the form CVC.CV (2c.1c), but this does not occur except in a few of the less favoured metres, and the necessity for assuming it has been disputed. The nuclei are separated from each other by one or more linking syllables ("ties", *sabab*, pl. *asbāb*) of a less well-determined character. One nucleus plus adjacent linking syllables constitutes a 'foot', and the traditional system describes these by appropriate patterns of the root *fᶜl* (hence the use *tafᶜīlah* for a foot). Two, three or four feet make a half-line or hemistich (*šaṭr*), and four, six or eight feet make the full 'line' (*bayt*).

The rhythmical pattern which identifies the particular metre of a poem is established by the nature of the first two feet of the hemistich; for, normally, a third foot is of the same type as the first, and a fourth of the same type as the second. However, the last foot of a hemistich, no matter how many feet precede it, may show a syllabic structure differing more substantially from that of the corresponding earlier foot than the minor variations which occur elsewhere than in the final foot of the hemistich. Poetry was always sung or chanted, and one can reasonably speculate that the style of singing may have been characterized (as is some Spanish folk-song today) by a drawn-out cadenza at the end of the melodic unit.

The following summary description of the nine most-used metres is given in two forms: that of the traditional *tafᶜīlāt*, with the nucleus syllables distinguished by capital letters (these being the invariable 'pegs' on which the whole metre depends); and a syllabic analysis of the kind used above. Most of the metres are easily describable and recognisable, but there are one or two where the traditional system is somewhat artificial as a result of excessive schematization. In two metres, *Kāmil* and *Wāfir*, the linking group of syllables has basically the form 1c.1c.2c, but provided that this basic form appears somewhere in the poem, it can arbitrarily be replaced in any position by the form 2c.2c [in this respect, these two metres bear some resemblance to Greek and Latin dactylic and anapaestic metres, with their optional variation between two short syllables and one long syllable]. In all other metres, the actual number of syllables in each linking group remains stable, but with the possibility that one position may be optionally filled either by a 2c or a 1c syllable [as with Greek tragic iambics, where in the odd-numbered feet of each line the first syllable may be either long or short]. These variable syllables are marked in the analysis as xc.

Kāmil: exemplified in this selection in pieces V, XV.

mu.ta.faa.^{c}I.LUN/mu.ta.faa.^{c}I.LUN

1c.1c.2c/ or 2c.2c/ 1C+2C/ 1c.1c.2c/ or 2c.2c/ 1C+2C/

Wāfir: exemplified in IX.

MU.FAA.^{c}i.la.tun/MU.FAA.^{c}i.la.tun

1C+2C/ 1c.1c.2c/ or 2c.2c/ 1C+2C/ 1c.1c.2c/ or 2c.2c/

Ṭawīl: exemplified in VII,XIV,XIX-XXII,XXIV,XXV,XXX,XXXIV,XXXV.

FA.^{c}UW.lu(n)/MA.FAA.^{c}i(y).lun

1C+2C.xc/1C+2C.xc.2c/

Basīṭ: exemplified in I,XII,XXXVIII,XXXI,XXXII,XXXVII.

mu(s).taf.^{c}I.LUN/fa(a).^{c}I.LUN

xc.2c.1C+2C/xc.1C+2C/

Ramal: exemplified in II,XVIII,XXIII,XXIX.

fa(a).^{c}I.LAA.tun/fa(a).^{c}I.LAA.tun

xc.1C+2C.2c/xc.1C+2C.2c/

Rajaz, exemplified in XXVI, and *Sarī^{c}* in IV,XIII, both have the same rhythm in the body of the line, namely

mu(s).ta(f).^{c}I.LUN/mu(s).ta(f).^{c}I.LUN

xc.xc.1C+2C/xc.xc.1C+2C/

The only reason for distinguishing them as separate metres lies in the traditional schematization. As a handy rule of thumb, one can say that if the hemistich contains three feet of which the third is in the form xc.1C+2C, it will be classed as *Sarī^{c}*; otherwise it is *Rajaz*.

K̲afīf, exemplified in III,VIII,X,XI,XXXVI, has the syllabic pattern

xc.1c.2c.2c.xc.2c.1c.2c

in its body, which it might seem natural to interpret as

fa(a).^{c}I.LAA.tun/mu(s).taf.^{c}I.LUN

xc.1C+2C.2c/xc.2c.1C+2C

but the traditional system, under pressure of its schematization, adopts the hypothesis of a 2C+1C nucleus and interprets the second foot as xc.2C+1C.2c.

Munsariḥ: exemplified in VI,XVI,XVII,XXVII,XXXIII.

This presents problems in analysis. The hemistich has twelve syllables,

xc.xc.1c.2c.2c.xc.2c.1c.2c.1c.1c.2c

and Wright interprets this as a four-foot *Basīṭ* rhythm distinguished only by reduction of the second foot to a single 2c syllable,

[xc.2c.1C+2C/xc.1C+2C/xc.2c.1C+2C/xc.1C+2C (*Basīṭ*)]

xc.xc.1C+2C/ 2c /xc.2c.1C+2C/1c.1C+2C (*Munsariḥ*)

But the traditional system does not allow for a foot of only one syllable, and its interpretation here is as a three-foot hemistich,

mu(s).ta(f).ᶜI.LUN/maf.ᶜu(w).LAA.TU/mus.taf.ᶜI.LUN

xc.xc.1C+2C/2c.xc.2C+1C/2c.2c.1C+2C

RHYME. The majority of early verse has a single monorhyme at the end of each full line; in a formal *qaṣīdah*, the same rhyme occurs at the end of the first hemistich of the whole poem. In another type of rhyme (called *mašṭūr*), the two hemistichs of each line rhyme with each other, but the rhyme changes from line to line; this form existed from early times, but did not become really popular until a later date, when it made possible the composition of long pieces of several hundred lines (see above) which could not have been done under the obligation of a single monorhyme throughout.

The rhyme consists in the final consonant of the last word (letters of prolongation being excluded from consideration), plus any phonetic elements which follow it, i.e. vowel or *sukūn*. A piece is often referred to in terms of its rhyming conconant, e.g. a piece with *l* as rhyming consonant is a *lāmiyya*. A third-person pronoun affix is regarded as part of the 'following phonetic elements' and does not alone constitute a rhyme: a *mīmiyya* poem may have the rhyme sequence *kirāmuhā* - *jimāmuhā* &c.

A long vowel immediately preceding the rhyme consonant, when the latter is itself vowelled, or a short vowel immediately preceding an unvowelled rhyme consonant, is subject to a restricted type of rhyme: an *a* quality vowel repeats without variation, but *i* and *u* quality vowels rhyme freely with each other: hence *ḍīq* + vowel rhymes with *sūq* + vowel, and *lam yujib* with *lam yatub*. If there is ā in the syllable next but one before the rhyme consonant, this also repeats, though the intervening consonant may change; for an example of this kind of rhyme see piece XXV here.

The last word of the line is in 'pause', inasmuch as it precedes a break in utterance, and is subject to the phonetic rules of pause. One of these is that in pause the syllabic structure CVCC, unacceptable within the stretch of connected discourse, is possible. But pause position does not permit the word to end in a short vowel; a naturally short vowel in this position is either replaced by *sukūn*, or lengthened by the addition of a letter of prolongation. Thus the final syllable of a line is obligatorily 2c (or, as just mentioned, 3c), but never 1c. Pause position further demands elimination of *tanwīn*. The normal forms *al-kitābu* and *kitābun* must at the end of the line be pronounced with a final syllable *-bū* in both cases. On the other hand, normal *sukūn* can in this position be replaced by *-ī*, as in *lam yujibī* "he did not reply".

It is specially important to be aware of a convention of script which applies in the writing of verse. The lengthening of naturally short *i* or *u* in pause must be pronounced but is not written; but the lengthening of *a* is written, with the consequence that, for example, the written form *kānā* at the end of a line may mean "he was" as well as "they two were".

LINGUISTIC FEATURES OF VERSE. There are various grammatical forms which are peculiar to verse, the most important being as follows.

1. The pronoun affixes *-ī*, *-nī* may, if the metrical structure so demands, have to be pronounced *-iya, -niya*.
2. The pronoun forms *hum, -hum, 'antum,-kum* have commonly in verse a final vowel added which may be long or short according to the demands of the metre, i.e. *humu, humū* (also *-himu, -himū, -himi, -himī*).
3. *wa* and *fa* in combination with *huwa, hiya* must often be pronounced *wahwa, wahya*.
4. The imperfect forms *yakun, takun, 'akun, nakun* may drop the *n* and appear as *yaku* &c.
5. By a phenomenon known as *tarḵīm*, the final syllable of a personal name may be dropped in the vocative; the resulting form may then be left as it is and undeclinable, or given case inflexion; hence *yā fāṭima / yā fāṭimu* for

yā fāṭimatu. Note therefore that *yā ᶜabdu* is not an address to a male slave, but to a lady named ᶜAbda(tu). In addition to personal names, *yā ṣāḥibu* may be shortened in verse to *yā ṣāḥi*. Analogous with this is the fact that (in prose as well as verse) *yā rabbī* "My Lord!" (addressed to God) is normally (*yā*) *rabbi* and so spelt.

6. Any diptote noun whatever may be freely used in verse as triptote, with full declension *-un, -an, -in* instead of the 'grammatical' *-u, -a*.

7. A feature which began to be common from Baššār's time onwards (though probably not wholly unattested earlier) is reduction of *-uwa, -iya* at the end of a word to *-ū, -ī*. E.g. *'ubdī* for *'ubdiya* "he was made to appear", and *al-qāḍī* for the accusative *al-qāḍiya*.

8. Elision of *hamz* at the end of the word also began to be not uncommon from the end of the second century, thus producing e.g. *al-ḵaṭā* for *al-ḵaṭa'u, al-ḵaṭa'a, al-ḵaṭa'i*; and as a further consequence *ḵaṭāya* "my fault" for *ḵaṭa'ī* (as in III, line 1).

9. Elision of *hamz* at the beginning of the word is common only in the juncture *law + 'anna*, producing *la.wan.na* (1c.2c.1c instead of 2c.2c.1c).

The student also needs to be aware of certain conventions of spelling which, while not specific to verse, are important in relation to the scanning (evaluation of the rhythms) of verse:

10. The isolated first person singular pronoun is spelt in a way which reflects its pause pronunciation; when not in pause it consists of two 1c syllables *'a.na* (unless of course followed by *hamzat al-waṣl*, when the first consonant of the following word must be syllabified with the pronoun, as in *'a.nal.mu.raᶜ.ᶜa.tu* "I am al-Muraᶜᶜat").

11. The plural demonstrative *'ulā* "those" is, when it forms the complete word, always spelt with a *wāw*, thus making it indistinguishable in writing from the feminine of "first", *'ūlā*. When it is a part of a longer form, such as *hā'ulā'i* and *'ulā'ika*, it is sometimes spelt with the *wāw*. But in all cases it must be pronounced and scanned with a short *u*.

12. The third person masculine singular affix pronoun, though always spelt *-hu/-hi*, is pronounced *-hū/-hī* after a short vowel and *-hu/-hi* after a long one (*bi-hī, fī-hi*). Similarly, even when the pronoun forms mentioned in 2 above have to be pronounced with a long vowel at the end, the vowel-length is not recorded in the spelling.

METAPHOR AND SIMILE. Metaphor, or the replacement of a 'proper' term by another with which it is compared (e.g. 'my honey' put in place of 'my beloved'), is ubiquitous in all language. But metaphors in everyday use have a constant tendency towards devaluation of their effect, right up to a point where they become 'dead metaphors' no longer felt as metaphors at all. Poets who wish to make a poetic impact must coin their own fresh metaphors; and this is a very significant feature of Abbasid poetry. But in poetry before Baššār's time, freshly-coined metaphors were rarely used, the poets in general preferring the figure of the simile, or explicit comparison by means of *k*- "like" ('my love is like honey').

There is, however, a form to which critics of English sixteenth and seventeenth century poetry have given the name 'extended simile'. In this, there is no one-to-one comparison between two single terms: the point of the comparison lies in the total picture presented by a phrase or sentence following the "like". This form is used in some of the Gospel parables, where the Authorised Version has 'the kingdom of heaven is like a man who ...': there is no intention here to say that the kingdom of heaven is like a man of any kind, but to use the following 'parable' (in which the man may be a wholly subordinate element) as illuminating or illustrating, in its total effect, the nature of the kingdom of heaven. Hence the New English Bible renders 'the kingdom of heaven is like this: a man ....'. Arabic extended similes are of the same type, and the sutudent needs to be on the look-out for them.

TRANSLATIONS AND COMMENTARY

Amatory Pieces

Muslim love-poetry is almost exclusively emotional and sentimental in tone; a frankly erotic piece like XVII here is a distinct rarity. Normally, the poet's theme is praise of the lady's charms of disposition (more than her physical beauties), and laments over his unrequited or frustrated passion. This attitude to some extent echoes a convention of the pre-Islamic bedouin *qaṣīdah* which, whatever its main topic may be, normally begins with a romantic passage (called the *nasīb*) in which the poet meditates nostalgically over the deserted traces of an encampment where, many years before, he had had a love affair with a girl who is now far away. Many of the stock allusions of the bedouin *nasīb* continue to crop up in urban Muslim poetry.

I

People said, 'Do you rave about one whom you cannot see?', but I replied, 'The ear, like the eye, may tell the heart of that which is'.

I am not the first one to be enamoured of a maiden, in whose encounter he encounters only a waft of perfume.

O folk, my ear has fallen in love with a maiden of the tribe, for sometimes the ear falls in love before the eye.

Sources: M 344; A iii.238; H^1 67, H^2 60. Metre: *Basīṭ*.

qaa.luw.BI.MAN/laa.TA.RAA/tah.d̲iy.FA.QUL/tu.LA.HUM

'al.'ud̲.NU.KAL/ᶜay.NI.TUW/fil.qal.BA.MAA/kaa.naa

1. Alluding to the poet's blindness. A glosses *tūfī* as *tubligu* "communicate".
2. I have taken *rawḥan* in the sense of "breeze", though it could alternatively be understood in its other sense (more common in modern Arabic) "refreshment".
3. Mention of the tribe is strictly speaking inappropriate in the urban context, but is not uncommon as an echo of the bedouin style.

II

My night was not long, yet I have not slept; a haunting phantom banished sleep from me.

If I say, 'Be generous to us', she takes refuge in silence, saying neither yea nor nay.

Grant me some respite, ᶜAbdah; and know, ᶜAbdah, that I am but flesh and blood.

Beneath my coat there is a wasted body; were you to lean on it, it would collapse.

5 Love for her has set a seal on my neck, in place of the *ḏimmī* seal.

Sources: M 329; A iii.151; H^1 70, H^2 62. Metre: *Ramal*.

lam.YA.ṬUL.lay/liy.WA.LAA.kin/lam.'A.NAM

wa.NA.FAA.ʿan/nil.KA.RAA.ṭay/fun/'A.LAMM

1. The idea is that although the poet did not sleep, the night did not seem long to him because the vision of the beloved was always before him.

5. At many periods in early Islam, a member of the non-Muslim protected minorities (a *ḏimmī*) was required to wear round his neck a leaden docket stamped with the certificate of payment of the poll-tax (*jizyah*). This allusion implies that the slavery of love is comparable with the inferior social status of the *ḏimmī*.

III

ʿAbdah, I confess my sin, so forgive, and set aside my fault.

ʿAbdah, I cannot endure any more; but soft! I do not say that you have reproached me with that which is no true reproach!

I said, when love wearied me, wasted my body, and tormented my heart,

'My Lord, I cannot endure separation; enough! grant me remission! enough! praise be to Thee! Enough!'

Sources: M 43; H^1 70, H^2 63. Metre: *Ḵafīf*.

ʿab.DU.'IN.niy/qa.diʿ/TA.RAF/tu.BI.ḎAN.biy

faḡ.FI.RIY.waʿ/ru.kiy.ḴA.ṬAA/ya.BI.JAN.biy

IV

ʿAbdah, visit me, and you will be a boon of God to me on the day when I meet with you.

I swear by God - be sure of this - that I long for you but fear you.

ʿAbdah, I perish and am lost if I taste not the cool touch of your lips;

do not reject a lover at death's door, who would be content with the least measure of that.

Sources: M 264; H^1 71, H^2 63. Metre: *Sarīʿ*.

yaa.^{c}ab.DA.ZUW/riy.niy.TA.KUN/min.NA.TAN

lil.laa.HI.^{c}IN/diy.yaw.MA.'AL/qaa.kiy

4. *hāḏā l-qadri* "this measure" is intended to be accompanied by a gesture indicating something small.

V

O my night, you grow ever more hateful, because of the love I bear towards a maiden with whom I have become enamoured.

A sparkling-eyed maiden is she; if she glances towards you, she makes you drunk with wine by those two eyes.

The pattern of her discourse seems like meadow plots garbed in flowers,

and as though beneath her tongue Harut sat breathing spells therein.

You might well imagine the body on which she gathers her garments to be all gold and scent.

It is as though she were the very coolness of drink itself - drink pure and suited to your breaking fast.

Be she a maiden of the jinn, a human girl, or somewhat between, she is a most splendid thing.

It is enough to say that I never heard tell of any complaint about the one I love,

save the cry of one who would visit her: 'She has scattered sorrows all around for me,

victim of passion for a ten-days space, and of very death for ten'.

Sources: M 165; A iii.155; H^1 72, H^2 64. Metre: *Kāmil*.

yaa.lay.LA.TIY/taz.daa.DU.NUK/ran

min.ḥub.BI.MAN/'aḥ.bab.TU.BAK/ran

3. *raj^{c}* is an echo of pre-Islamic usage in which it is applied to the pattern of tattooing, in lines running 'backward and forward'.

4. Hārūt was a legendary magician.

9. The 'one who would visit her' is the poet himself, frustrated in his desire of seeing her.

10. *mutaḵaššī^{c}an* is a circumstantial accusative referring to the pronoun contained in *lī. ^{c}ašran* scil. "nights" (hence the feminine form); periods of time in early Arabic usage were commonly reckoned in terms of nights in preference to days.

VI

O my two friends, for this evening be charitable: love is a serious thing for a man, and no sport.

By God, by God, I do not sleep, and cannot withhold my eye from its tears of sorrow.

Fate has made to endure for us a memory of one who was near but is now distant and remote.

How grievous are my tears, that I may not speak to her as on the day she departed, wending her way in distant paths.

What was my crime, that I have been tormented by her? What unlucky star was for us cause of grief?

I have exhausted my tears over the beloved, and have amazed my folk; yet I am no marvel —

man before me has been befooled by passion, and carried away by the love of girls, whether that love be chaste or deceitful.

My love for Salmā and for the sight of her has been truly a mote sticking in my tear-ducts:

I desire to forget her, but then am reminded of her by the qualities ever present in my two ladies.

How strange is Salmā: she cannot endure the one who gossips about us, while I cannot endure the one who reproaches me for loving her.

In memory she is near, whenever she is absent, so that I behold her person though it is not near.

And on the day when I was complaining to Usāmah of the secret depth of my passion, and it flared up and blazed,

dear Salmā said, 'Are we then neglectful of you? But you do not know how to milk the udder well;

respect a friend and you will win respect from him; but you will never gather grapes from his thorns'.

O adornment of womankind, you have been created of wondrous stuff; lust for forbidden things comes swiftly and brings good conduct to shame.

But with pure heart, while envious eyes were present which have forecast for us every sunrise direst consequences,

she made a stealthy sign with her fingertips to me, to tell me of her feelings; and they stirred up my passion, although maybe they lied.

Thus did she act, but then she turned away — just as I called on resolution to aid me, but it turned away.

How many a joy there is of which we have tasted the pleasure; but how many too an assembly, the memory of which has turned to weariness.

Nothing remains but the phantom of her, reminding me of what was, and was so eagerly desired.

Abandon all thought of Salmā; she is a grief to him who pursues her; human plans will not win the race without destiny's aid.

I will leave love's folly to other eyes; but I will not abandon the quaffing of ruddy wine and the cup.

Sources: D i.323; H^1 72, H^2 64. Metre: *Munsariḥ*.

yaa.ṣaa.ḤI.BAY/yal.^{c}a.ŠIY.YA/taḥ.ta.SI.BAA

jad.dal.HA.WAA/bil.fa.TAA.WA/maa.la.^{c}I.BAA

1. This common use of the verb *iḥtasaba* originates from the expression *iḥtasaba 'ajra l-'āḵirati* "he reckoned on the reward of the world to come", and has then come to be used, with omission of the object, in the sense of "perform a charitable deed" (such as enables one to reckon on being rewarded for it in the future life).

3. There is an echo here and in the following line of the pre-Islamic theme of the beloved whose tribe has migrated so that her lover can no longer meet her.

4. D has the vocalization *sulāf* "wine", but as the D edd. point out, this is wholly inappropriate to the context, and they conjecture *silāf* as a plural of *salīf* "path".

9. *jārah* is the normal polite word for a wife in bedouin language. *muktasab* properly describes an acquired characteristic as contrasted with an innate one (*jibillah*), but no special emphasis rests on the contrast here.

10. *nuṭī^{c}u* is by poetic license for the singular, referring to the poet, not to the two lovers together; for there is a rhetorical contrast between the lady whose chief fear is the *wāšī*, and the lover whose chief enemy is the *^{c}ātibah*.

13. "knowing how to milk the udder" is a proverbial expression for being

able to handle a situation successfully.

14. "His thorns" implies, if you have made him 'prickly' by ill-treating him.

16. *^{c}ayyanna* here is made to govern two accusatives.

21. The D ms. in fact reads *al-rā'idūna*, which D comm. declares to be a corruption, and the D edd. print (as does H) the reading given in my text. In a footnote, however, the D edd. admit that the ms. reading is possible; it would yield the rendering "those who seek pasturage (i.e. cherish longings) cannot outstrip what is decreed by fate".

VII

That which you know has increased my yearning for you, and my sorrowing heart is all a-flutter.

Mention is never made of you without tears starting to my eye for love of you.

All night long my eye is in thrall to tears, and in the morning I am a lover with heart distressed.

When the people speak, sitting in conclave, I am bowed down as though I were a stranger among them all,

while they say, 'Heart-sickness is a demon which has afflicted him': but my sickness is a gazelle brought up in the bowers.

At any time, a waft of the south wind can stir up my love for you, a love inspired by tenderness;

it is the north wind, when it blows, that is my companion's longing, but for my own heart's sake I long for the south wind to blow,

and that is because when it comes, it comes laden with the scent of dear ^{c}Abdah.

I seek dear ^{c}Abdah as my remedy; she, however I may conceal it, is physician for my sickness.

Like the phial of the druggist, or more than that, is her likeness; soft is she and sweet, when I upbraid her.

Dear ^{c}Abdah has engaged my heart in passion; no other lady has any part in my soul.

Forbear, for God's sake, to slay a lover, whose evening hours are full of sighs and weeping;

one who sunders his affection from his nearest and dearest, since he has no kinsman save longing for you.

When you are far away, you make me long for the lucky chance of meeting you; but when near, you cheat me of my due.

I do not know, by God, whether dear ^{c}Abdah will deny our love, or requite and reward it.

I am the most wretched of men if my love for her flourishes, while that on which it should feed is barren.

Many a one there is who says, 'If you die in pursuit of passion, sins must be reckoned against you,

so seek repentance before the moment of death, for I fear God's wrath against you when you come to your last hour',

thus taking it upon herself to guide me, and that at a time when my hair has grown gray, and my folk lay their burdens upon me, and I am one in whom there is no lack of confidence;

to such a one I reply, 'I have committed no fault against anyone in the love which is between us, so for what should I repent?'

I see that we are close neighbours, and meet often, yet are never alone, strange as that is:

would that I knew whether I may visit you some time with no jealous eye to watch over us, dear ^{c}Abdah,

so might we cure our hearts of their longing desire, since the lover's cure is the beloved.

If I forget anything else of what is brought forth for a man by fate, and by its varying chances which befall him,

yet I'll not forget the taste of the moisture of your lips, even when the sunset of my life's day is near.

I live through the night for the love wherewith you have fed me, and it is as though I were stripped of family and ancestral wealth.

Though I may say, 'The closing of my eye for a space will make me forget you', still my fears and sorrows will be plain to you.

Sources: D i.178; (M 15, lines 7.8.4); H^1 67, H^2 60; R 38 ff. Metre: *Tawīl*.

LA.QAD.zaa/DA.NIY.maa.ta^c/LA.MIY.na/ṢA.BAA.ba.tan

'I.LAY.ki/FA.LIL.qal.bil/ḤA.ZIY.ni/WA.JIY.buw

4. It is the privilege of the tribal member, but not of a stranger to the tribe, to speak at the tribal conclave. The poet depicts himself as so much preoccupied with his love that he has nothing to say about tribal affairs and sits speechless with downcast eyes as if he were an alien in the tribe.

5. The distracted lover is often represented as *majnūn* "possessed by a jinn", i.e. mad. *rabīb* is an animal brought up as a pet in the tent or house; there is a rhetorical contrast between the hideous and terrifying image of the jinn and the delicate mild pet.

6. *'iḏā ši'tu* is in Baššār's language a cliché which has been drained of its proper meaning ("whenever I wish") and signifies nothing more than "at any time"; this can be seen most clearly in the last line of XIX, where the rendering "whenever I wish" would make nonsense.

D prints the vocalization *šawqu,* as subject of *hāja* used intransitively, and R follows this. This, however, is impossible, since it leaves *hubūbu* at the end of the line without any verb (R's rendering "au [*sic*] souffle du vent" is equally impossible with the nominative). We must read *šawqa* as object to *hāja* used transitively, with *hubūbu* as its subject; *wa qtādahū l-hawā* is then parenthetical, as the punctuation provided in H implies. Although *šawq* and *hawā* are commonly used indifferently by amatory poets, there is properly a distinction between them: *hawā* is a less intense feeling than *šawq*, but is a necessary preliminary stage which then leads on (*iqtāda*) to *šawq.*

12. The phrase *ittaqi llāha* "fear God" is a conventional formula used when begging a person *not* to do a thing. The imperative is here replaced by the imperfect indicative, a common feature of urbanized polite language. *'alā* is an expletive which may be prefixed to a request whether phrased in the imperative or in the indicative.

16. The footnote in H, identifying *murtād* as an active participle, is wrong; it is the passive form used as a noun of place, "pasture ground". *janāb* is the tract of ground adjacent to an encampment or settlement (see Lane), and the genitive is one of identity, 'the *janāb* which is a pasture ground'. The D comm. queries the reading, and proposes emending to *jinān* "gardens", but this hardly seems an effective improvement.

19. A person 'on whom burdens are laid' is in bedouin language a stock

expression for a senior man of the tribe. The same is the implication of the phrase at the end of the line. *laysa* can be used indeclinably, as a simple substitute for *lā*.

27. D prints as alternatives the vocalizations *ta^{c}arraḍa* and *ta^{c}arraḍu*; R has opted for the former, H for the latter. My own preference is for the latter; the imperfect indicative being justified by the fact that the clause is not logically conditioned - what it states will be so no matter whether or not the poet utters the sentiment given in the first part of the line. *lakum* is something of a problem. At first sight, R's rendering "craintes, angoisses t'assailleraient" (with *-kum* for *-ki* by poetic license) seems grammatically the most natural; yet it runs counter to the trends of amatory poetry, in which the fears and miseries are virtually always felt by the lover, rather than the beloved. Moreover, if it was ^{c}Abdah who experienced the fears, we would have to envisage her taking seriously the idea that the poet might actually sleep and forget her; yet the first hemistich clearly implies that because sleep brings forgetfulness, the poet cannot sleep, and the second hemistich would then describe his sleepless situation, beset by anxieties on behalf of ^{c}Abdah. This suggests that it is the poet's fears which 'present themselves' (i.e. are apparent) to her.

VIII

You two cupbearers, pour out my drink, and give me a draught of the moist lips of a delicate fair maiden;

my sickness is thirst, my remedy a drink from a cool moist mouth.

She has a smile like the shining petals of the camomile, a speech like embroidery, the embroidery of cloaks.

She has settled in the inmost recesses of my heart's core, and has won even more than that, like one importunate.

Then she said, 'We will meet you some nights hence': but the passage of nights will wear out every new thing.

She can rest content without meeting me: but my lot is sighs which eat away a heart of iron.

Sources: M 109; D ii.272; A iii.187; H^{1} 71, H^{2} 63. Metre: *Ḵafīf*.

'ay.YU.HAL.saa/qi.YAA.NI.ṣub/baa.ŠA.RAA.biy

was.QI.YAA.niy/min.RIY.QI.bay/ḍaa.'A.RUW.diy

3. The camomile flower is proverbial for whiteness.

IX

When the oryx-herd shows gleaming, I remember Salmā, and I remember her when the musk-bag wafts its scent.

It is as though you had never visited other maidens with their sparkling teeth, and your passionate soul had never foregathered with them.

The lover is terrified by whispering on any matter, for fear that the whispering should be concerned with him;

his heart is as it were a ball bouncing about, for anxious fear of separation — would that anxiety could be of any use!

I say, as my night lengthens out, 'When they are gone, will night have any daybreak?'

His eyelids are as though pierced with a sharp thorn, and no sleep for him can find an abiding place in them.

My eye has become a stranger to slumber, so that its eyelids seem too short for it.

Sources: M 153; H^1 71, H^2 63. Metre: *Wāfir*.

'I.ḎAA.laa.ḥal/ṢU.WAA.ru.ḏa.kar/TU.SAL.maa

WA.'AḎ.ku.ru.haa/'I.ḎAA.na.fa.ḥal/ṢU.WAA.ruw

1. Two senses of *ṣuwār* are punningly employed. The oryx (a type of gazelle frequenting sand desert and characterized by a brilliantly white colour) is a stock image in poetry for a beautiful woman.
2. The poet here turns to addressing himself.
7. *jafā ᶜan* literally "slide off".

X

Long was my night by reason of love for one who I think will not be close to me

ever, so long as starlight shows to your eye,

or a singing-girl chants an ode in a drinker's hearing.

I sought to find solace apart from dear ᶜAbdah, but love is too strong

for me.
Were the love of that lady for sale, I would purchase it with all my wherewithal,
and were I but able at will to influence fate's decrees,
I and mine should ransom her from death
My darling made complaint — for the love-lorn is full of complaints —
of a rumour which a liar's word reported to her:
then I tossed sleepless, with my hairs starting on end,
for amazement at her coldness — but passion begets amaze —
and with tears clothing my breast I said,
'Were I to abandon hope of dear ^{c}Abdah, my knell would have rung'.
^{c}Abdah, for God's sake release from continuing torment
a man who was, before meeting you, a monk or as good as one,
who lay sleepless all night long, looking for things to come,
but was then turned away from his devotions by passion for a full-breasted maiden,
who with love of herself drove the Great Judge's reckoning out of his mind;
he is a lover whose heart will not recant from loving her,
and who complains of a sting like a scorpion's in his breast,
for suchlike is what the lover experiences at the mention of beloved.
Fear grips me that my kinsfolk may bear my coffin
all too soon, before I behold in you any relenting.
So if you hear one of my kinswomen weeping,
and amid those clad in garments of woe lamenting a martyr to maidens,
then know that love for you has brought me to destruction.

Sources: D 1.163; R 26 ff. Metre: *K̲afīf*.

ṭaa.LA.LAY.liy/min.ḤUB.BI.man

laa.'U.RAA.hu/mu.QAA.RI.biy

1. *'urāhu* literally "I am shown so-and-so" = "it seems to me that".

4. R reads *mā ta^{c}azzaytu*, with a full stop at the end of line 1, and *'abadan* in line 2 qualifying the verb in line 4, "never could I find solace". This emendation of the D text is unnecessary: the full stop should be placed

at the end of line 3, and *'abadan* taken with line 1.

6. R takes *ṭā'i*^{c}*an* in the sense of "while I am subject to her", on the basis of the primary sense of the verb *ṭā*^{c}*a* "be submissive". However, the participial form *ṭā'i*^{c}*an* is commonly used in a specialized sense, namely "willingly, of one's own accord" as antithesis to *kārihan* "unwillingly, under constraint", and I would suppose this to be meant here.

7. *hārib wa-qārib* is a bedouin expression meaning "he who comes away from the watering-place and he who is going down to it", i.e. everybody; here, therefore, implying 'everybody belonging to me'.

XI

Su^{c}dā's kiss, Ibn al-Dujayl, is remedy, so let me taste of it; every sickness has one cure.

My friends have slept oblivious of me; I know not sleep, for in my eye there is a grit and in my heart a sickness.

The gossips say, 'You love Su^{c}dā', and they tell the truth; by the High God, my love is past cure.

I seem not to live, now that my darling has departed and enemies surround my dwellings;

my tender true friend has gone, and he who is hateful is now neighbour of my dwelling: this is a sore distress.

She was close to me for a while, like water, but when she had departed Harran was waterless.

Come now, journey through night and day to a bright-eyed girl — though in her is waywardness and perversity —

and take comfort from your beloved in all you encounter; everything save the beloved is mere vexation.

The physician says, 'Only in God's mercy is any avail; I have none to offer'.

It is a light thing, so long as you yourself are safe, to suffer the loss of someone (what soul has that which it desires in unmixed measure?)

in the endurance of separation from whom no affliction need be felt, for with lapse of time solace will come to you.

The target of misfortunes is never safe: his every cup has only dregs.

31

Source: D i.113. Metre: *K̲afīf.*

riy.QU.SU^{c}.daa/yab.NAL.DU.jay/lil.ŠI.FAA.'uw

fas.QI.NIY.hi/li.KUL.LI.daa/'in.DA.WAA.'uw

4. *lā 'urānī* see note on X.1. The last syllable of *ḥibbu* belongs metrically to the second hemistich, which therefore has to be scanned

bu.WA.ḤAF.fat/bu.YUW.TI.yal/'a^{c}.daa.'uw

The reduction of the last foot to three 2c-syllables occurs also in line 12.

6. The poet spent some time in Harran, under the patronage of the Umayyad prince Sulaymān b.Hišām b.^{c}Abd al-Malik, to whom piece XXXV is addressed. The point about 'like water' is that rainwater, though a grateful refreshment to the parched land, soon dries up.

7. *ṣil* "join" night and day in one continuous march.

9. I.e., his disease (love) is incurable.

10. This and the next line, as vocalized in the D text, present problems of identifying the pronoun references. The D edd. ingeniously (perhaps too much so) suggest the possibility that the two lines are still part of the doctor's words to the poet, and in order to achieve this they propose the vocalization *salimta* ... *^{c}alayka*, and emending the ms. *yablā* to *tablā*. In this case, the doctor (like the conventional 'reproacher') is urging the poet to regard the loss of his beloved as something that time will enable him to get over. My own inclination is not to accept this, but to retain the text vocalization with the two pronouns feminine and addressed to the beloved; in which case the *faqīd* is, as the D comm. proposes, the poet himself, who will have died of love. This interpretation does, however, require the vocalization *yublā* (impersonal passive) instead of the D text *yablā* (for which there is no available subject if the poet is addressing Su^{c}dā).

XII

K̲uššābah, has any lover joy of you or not? For I am struggling in the toils of death;

were all mankind beset by what I am, unable to reach their loves, they would have perished.

Separation has a fire which ravages my heart and breast when you are far away, but the sight of your face is cooling as ice.

My love for you, when I would conceal it, seems abyss on abysses, above me and below my feet,

so I proclaim my love, unable to struggle against its mightiness; as for you, it is as though candle were hidden below bushel.

Kuššābah, be generous, whether openly or by stealth, for I am worn out and years have passed over my hopes.

How long, Kuššābah, will you stay unmoving, neither at any time coming out to us, nor we entering to you?

If you had experienced what we do, you would ordain for us a day whereon we might gain life from you and rejoice;

there is no good in life if we are to be always thus, never meeting, though the path to meeting is plain and straight.

He who keeps his eye on other men will never win his want; it is the bold swashbuckler who carries off the fair prizes.

You have been forbidden to meet me by certain people (may they never know an untroubled life, never lack an adversary — and never win!)

who say our meeting is a sinful thing; but they lie, for there is no peril in a clinging embrace or a kiss.

Do you not know, sweet girl, that I have no joy apart from the longing which you have inspired in me?

I bid my soul rejoice whenever my eye twitches, and I say, 'It has twitched in token of my gaining you'.

I have longed to meet you some day in private, but how can that be, since there is waywardness in what you say to me?

I make complaint to God of a passion which does not forsake me, and of distracted thoughts which pervade my inmost heart.

Lord, I cannot endure without being close to a maiden who from waywardness keeps herself afar, and who even when she is near proves coy;

beauteous, sparkling-eyed, made of scent when she breathes; the room and the whole house have a perfume from her breath;

she is like a moon full-rounded, sweet of smile and black of eye.

33

Source: D ii.74. Metre: *Basīṭ*.

k̲uš.šaa.BA.HAL/li.MU.ḤIB/bin.^{c}in.DA.KUM/fa.RA.JUW

'aw.laa.FA.'IN/niy.BI.ḤAB/lil.maw.TI.MU^{c}/ta.LI.JUW

5. There is an evident echo here of the Gospel expression (Mat.5.15), 'Neither do men light a candle, and put it under a bushel, but on a candlestick; and it giveth light unto all that are in the house'. The plural *suruj* is simply a poetic license for the singular *sirāj*, and it may be noted that although the English version has 'candle', the Syriac Gospel version has *s'rāgā* "lamp", the exact equivalent of the Arabic word. The figure is an 'extended simile' (see Introduction): that is, the poet is not comparing K̲uššābah to a bushel, but her circumstances to the total picture presented in the simile. The D edd. (no doubt unfamiliar with the Gospel) propose emending *ṣā^{c}* to *ṣubḥ*. This certainly yields a sentiment very common both in amatory and in eulogistic verse, "you are like dawn, beneath which lamps pale into insignificance". But there is very little resemblance of form between the two words in writing, such as might lead to a corruption; and it is really hardly conceivable that any copyist, if he had the simple word 'dawn' in front of him, which is very common in verse, should have written down,instead of it,'bushel'.

13. *fadatki l-nafsu jāriyatan* "may my life be a ransom for you as a girl" is one of the many elaborations of the 'ransom' theme used in Abbasid times as a polite salutation.

14. It was a popular belief that a twitching of the eye was a good omen presaging success in love.

16. *šurra^{c}* is plural of *šāri^{c}*, here used, as the D edd. suggest, of things which penetrate (*šara^{c}a fī*) the mind.

19. *rābin rawāfiduhū* "with swelling buttocks" implies a full moon, and the full moon is a stock Arabic image for a beautiful face.

XIII

Greet the dwelling-place in Ḏū Tanḍub, in Šaṭṭ Ḥawḍā, and in the sand tract of Qa^{c}nab,

and call on the riders to halt at its traces — or rather, to abide at that trace and not ride on.

Many a fellow armoured in health, who would not drink the antidote for a scorpion's sting,

who shuns fair maidens, and when it is morning neither weeps nor rejoices over any lady's dwelling,

have I wheedled out of the harshness of his manners by the sweetness of mine, without resorting to strife;

until, when passion has laid its grasp upon us, and he has become cheerful, in playful mood,

I have freely disclosed to him my love, and spoken in truth to him of Suʿdā and Zaynab,

saying, while a tear-drop wells in my eye unchecked,

'Though the dwelling and its inhabitants pass away, that which is in my heart will not pass away.

There is no marvel to compare with the dwelling of our folk, where the tawny lions and the oryx-herds step,

which was frequented by Suʿdā and her companions in the shade of a life of wondrous ease;

but now a sore time has passed over us, after a time which was not so,

and has snatched away Suʿdā altogether, save for the relicts of her compliant love'.

I have said to one who would ask about her love, when he had come close in the privilege of intimacy,

'My friend, do not ask of my love for her, but look upon my body and be amazed

at one wasted in frame, were you to measure him, one who made a passing impression on her heart but never entwined himself therein'.

I am infatuated with Suʿdā, present with us in sleep, though in reality she is one neither near nor accessible:

she is a Meccan woman, who when she goes out into the desert appears in the soft sands of Naʿmān or Maḡrib.

I have clung to a deceptive dream of her; would that that dream were not deceptive!

35

Sources: D i.145; H[1] 65, H[2] 58. Metre: *Sarīᶜ*.

sal.lim.ᶜA.LAL/daa.ri.BI.D̲IY/tan.Ḍ̣U.BIY

fa.šaṭ.ṬI.ḤAW/ḍaa.fa.LI.WAA/qaᶜ.NA.BIY

1,2. These lines are a variation on the conventional romantic preface (*nasīb*) of the *qaṣīdah*. The lavish use of geographical names is characteristic of bedouin poetry, and is intended to evoke in the hearer's mind a vivid reminiscence of the desert scene; Robert Browning uses Italian place-names in exactly the same way, for their evocative quality.

4. The person here described is pictured as being devoid of romantic feeling, and consequently the antithesis of the poet, with his nostalgic sorrow for past joys of love. Since *ṭarab* is applicable to any strong emotion, whether of joy or sorrow, the last word in the line could alternatively mean "sorrows".

8. *ḡuṣṣatun min ᶜabratin* lit. an obstruction consisting in a tear-drop.

10. *lā ḡarwa* is a hyperbolical expression implying 'there is nothing which can truly be called a wonder except ...'. *rubd* is the plural of the colour word *'arbad* applied conventionally to lions or ostriches. H has taken it to be here the latter, since it is a commonplace of the *nasīb* for the poet to stress that the former encampment is now tenanted only by wild beasts; on the reference to oryxes see note to IX.1. The D edd. on the other hand take *rubd* as meaning lions, and suppose the two words to be metaphors for the young men and girls of the tribe; in which case, the verb would have to be taken, like the verb in the next line, as referring to the past when the encampment was inhabited, whereas H would see a 'now and then' contrast in the two lines. *tamšī* seems to be an emendation of H, for the D text has *tumsī* "go about in the evening", which to my mind is less attractive.

13. *ḥad̲āfīr* is the top parts and sides of anything, and preceded by *bi-* "with" is a cliché phrase implying "altogether".

14. *fī ḥurmati l-'aqrabi* lit. the privileged position of the close kinsman.

18. The two places mentioned are in the vicinity of Mecca. There is an echo in this line of a line in the *Muᶜallaqah* of the pre-Islamic poet Labīd, who in deploring the inaccessibility of his beloved says *murriyyatun ḥallat bi-fayd ... fa-'ayna minka marāmuhā* "she is a Murrite girl, who has settled in Fayd ... so how can you hope for her?".

XIV

^{c}Abdah has a dwelling, but that dwelling speaks not to us; yet her abodes gleam bright as lines of writing;

I put my question to stones and a crumbled tent-trench, but how can trench and stones answer speech?

Her dwelling spoke not to me when I questioned it; while in my breast is as it were naphtha set aflame.

Could they but speak, many a tale would the abodes of her dwelling have for a sorrowful lover, whose passion is all too plain.

Sources: M 140; H^1 70, H^2 62. Metre: *Ṭawīl*.

LI.^{c}AB.da/TA.DAA.run.maa/TA.KAL.la/MU.NAAL.daa.ruw

TA.LUW.ḥu/MA.ḠAA.niy.haa/KA.MAA.laa/ḤA.'AS.ṭaa.ruw

The fire-blackened stones which have supported a cooking-pot, the tent-trench marking the place where a tent once stood, and the inability of these relics to tell the poet where the beloved is now, are all conventional themes in the bedouin *nasīb*.

XV

O lovely vision which I beheld in the face of a girl, for which I would have gone ransom!

She sent to me, offering for sale, the garment of love, but I have folded it away.

By God, Muḥammad's Lord, I never broke faith, nor thought of doing so.

I have held myself aloof from you, my lady; many a time has love's torment offered itself, and I have not desired it

The Caliph has forbidden — and when he forbids a thing, I too forbid it.

Many a one stained with henna, with slender fingers, has wept over me, and I have not wept for her.

The dwelling of the beloved was wont to inspire me with passion when I remembered it, but where is that dwelling now?

The Caliph stands guard over it, and I must endure without it, though I hate it not;

the hero-king has forbidden me to utter laments of love, and I have not disobeyed him.

Sources: D ii.24; M 68; H^{1} 74, H^{2} 66. Metre: *Kāmil*.

yaa.man.ẒA.RAN/ḥa.sa.nan.RA.ʼAY/tuh

min.waj.HI.JAA/ri.ya.tin.FA.DAY/tuh

Observe that the rhyming hemistichs of this piece have a single 2c syllable in place of the third foot, but the non-rhyming ones terminate at the end of the second foot.

The great influence which Baššār's love-poetry gained over the populace induced the Caliph Mahdī to interdict him from continuing to compose it; this piece is a renunciation by the poet in compliance with the Caliph's order, though the nature of the piece is such as to lead one to suspect that the renunciation was an ironic formality.

XVI

By God, were it not for the Caliph's good pleasure, I would not have done violence to myself under any stress.

But ill is often the lot chosen for men, and passion molests his frame.

So drink, in spite of time's cross-grainedness, for you will find no time free from cross-grained patches.

God gives you of His bounties, but man must endure the rubs when they come.

I have lived my life with myrtle, wine and flute, in the comfort of a fine hall;

and I have filled the lands, from the Fağfūr's realm to Kairouan and Yemen,

with poetry to which maidens and matrons pray as devoutly as the deluded heathen to their idol.

But then Mahdī forbade me, and my soul turned away from love-songs, as an honest prudent man would do.

Praise be to God, with Whom there is no partner; nothing remains steadfast against time.

Sources: A iii.241; M 367; H^{1} 75, H^{2} 67. Metre: *Munsariḥ*.

wal.laa.HI.LAW/laa.ri.ḌAAL.KA/liy.fa.TI.MAA

ʼa^{c}.ṭay.TU.ḌAY/man.^{c}a.LAY.YA/fiy.ša.JA.NIY

4. *yuḡḍī ʿaynan*, "blink (scil. over a grit, *qaḏā*)" = put up with discomfort.
6. Faḡfūr is an arabicization of Sanskrit *bhagapura* "son of god", itself a calque on the Chinese *t'ien-tzu* "son of heaven", the traditional official title of the emperor of China.
7. *ṯīb*, anomalous plural (as if from *ṯaybāʾu*) of *ṯayyib*.
9. In early Abbasid times, particularly among non-Arabs, *al-ḥamdu lillāh* came to be used as a phrase of pious resignation in misfortune, though this was contrary to correct Arab usage; there is a story in Tanūḵī's *Faraj* (ed. of 1955, p.240) in which the Caliph Rašīd reproves the vizier Jaʿfar b.Yaḥyā al-Barmakī for using it in this way. The concluding sentence of this piece, on the transitoriness of human affairs, shows that it is being used so here.

XVII

ʿUmar blamed me over my girl-friend (blame for no real reason is a vexatious thing),

'Come to your senses', said he, but I replied 'No!'; then he said, 'Yes, the tale of you two is in everyone's mouth'.

'If so,' said I, 'what excuse can I offer for something in which they will admit no excuses of mine?

I'll not hide from men my love for one who slays me; no, no, and again no! I hate what they say;

but blame me if you like — after this love affair with her there will be no occasion for blame, since your friend will be, by God, at point of death.

Be off with you! Be off, and tell them he refuses their advice and says, no, he will not "come to his senses", so be hanged to them!'.

What can any of them possibly say, seeing that this is a passion which fate has brought to fruition?

Folks, what have I ever to do with such people? It is an arrogant man who casts his eye on another's weakness.

Odd, very odd is this quarrel! May stones stop up the mouths of those who blame a man for love!.

Nobody who truly believes in God has ever blamed a lover; so be off! they are mere heathen.

39

For me and for her with whom I am in love it is enough to talk together and to gaze on each other,

or to kiss meanwhile (no harm in that, so long as there is no loosening of *my* garment),

or to feel with my hand beneath her dress while the door is discreetly curtained,

or a love-bite on her arm while mine too is marked by her teeth,

and while the anklets on her leg flash out, and the sound of panting breath is loud,

and her hand droops coyly, and with streaming tears she says, 'Let me alone!

go away, you are not like they said — you are, I swear, a wild fellow to deal with!

Nurse is away today, and has left you alone, so I have only God's help in dealing with you.

Lord, take my part! You see that I am too frail for this fellow with his licentious hand (yet he is not drunk);

a powerful fellow with a strength that nobody can stand up to has grasped at my bangle and crushed it,

pressing against me his rough black beard *which pricks* like needles,

so that he has overmastered me, while my family are away; shame upon them — had they been here

I swear by God you would not have escaped with your life. Go away! You are too brutal and overbearing.

How will my mother feel when she sees my lip, or if this tale about you gets around?

Or how, but how, will my nurse feel towards me? if only, if only prudence had been of any use!

I was from the first afraid of what I have suffered from you; but what can I say, you bold fellow?'.

At this, I said to her, 'My darling, all is well; I am experienced and prudent;

tell them *it was only* a gnat with claws (if there are gnats with claws!)'.

Sources: D iii.169; A iii.183. Metre: *Munsariḥ*.

qad.laa.MA.NIY/fiy.ka̱.LIY.LA/tiy.ᶜu.MA.RUW

wal.law.MU.FIY/ḡay.ri.KUN.HI/hiy.ḍa.JA.RUW

5. *lāmā* is the conventional address to two people (see Introduction). "Your friend" is the poet himself.

15. The first part of the line implies that her leg is bared. In the second hemistich A has *'aw maṣṣu rīqin wa-qad ᶜalā l-buḥuru* "or taste of kissing while there is loud panting"; *buḥur* is for *buḥr* (metrical license).

17. *muᶜārikun* is D's reading, A has *muḡāzilun* "flirter".

19. D has *al-šukuru(*I.e. *šukr*, see above), the idea of which is that gratitude for God's gifts implies obeying His laws, so that a person devoid of gratitude is one of whom one might say in English 'having no fear of God in him'. The D edd. characterize the A reading, which I have adopted, as a corruption; but it is viable, implying that the man's licentious conduct has not even the excuse of his being drunk.

23. The pronoun in *bihā* has to be understood as implying *nafsika*. If D's *musawwar* is correct, it means "endowed with brute force (*sawrah*)"; but A has *musāwir* "aggressor".

25. This line not in A, nor the following one in D.

26. The last word is an abbreviation of the bedouin expression *ᶜabru 'asfārin* "strong and bold in journeying".

27. *sakan* "rest" is applied to a person in whose company one is relaxed and at ease.

XVIII

The bones of dear Salmā my love are sugarcane, not bones of camel;
if you bring an onion close to her, the musk scent overpowers the onion stench.

Source: A iii.156. Metre: *Ramal*.

'in.NA.MAA.ᶜaẓ/mu.SU.LAY.maa/ḥib.BA.TIY

qa.ṢA.BUL.suk/ka.RI.LAA.ᶜaẓ/mul.JA.MAL

Baššār (like Euripides and Wordsworth) has been criticized for sometimes falling into bathos in his striving for homely phraseology. A quotes this as an example.

***

Elegiac and moralizing pieces

XIX

Lady, sink not under grief, but turn to God for comfort: to me also there has come my share of fell death,

for, to my despite and vexed sorrow, I have been afflicted with the death of my dear son; his living presence has been changed for stones and grave-wall.

I seem to be a stranger in life since the death of Muḥammad, and after him death is no stranger among us.

I must endure with longsuffering the loss of the best of youths; I have been afflicted thereby, and were it not for my reverence for God, long would have been my lament.

By my life, I would have defended Muḥammad from death, if it had been that the fates would forbear for a physician.

Yet why should I despair for one who has indeed passed away, but the blow of whose loss is a common experience? and for his coming to fountains that I too must taste.

So now I show a brave face to all eyes — but, o hapless heart smitten for his sake!

Every day I have a wellspring of tears that I do not pour out, that I may win the grace of longsuffering, or the putting off of sins.

The fates called to him, and he answered their voice; how fearful are both caller and answerer!

I cease not to tremble before the assaults of fate, as though my heart were pinned to the wing of a questing bird.

I marvel at how swiftly fate has moved towards him; it would have been no marvel if I had been granted a longer lease of his life.

I have been afflicted with the loss of my dear son, at a time when his wood was in full leaf, while upon me every kinsman cast his care;

yet I had hoped that Muḥammad would be to us a sufficient defence, whether as warrior or as spokesman.

His being was like the scent of a bride; but he withered away after a gladsome budding and sweetness, noble-browed, long-armed, a valiant hero, like the champion's sword brandished in no idle threat.

A vanguard party of us set forth in the morning, and a late starter travelled in the heat of the day in the tracks of the earlier ones, led along like a trace-horse.

We are all just like the jostling crowd that has gone before, victims of a fate which sometimes misses the mark and sometimes strikes home.

We pin our hopes to a life which is but wretched, which makes sore assaults on our bodies and souls.

But what is the good of a life that is ever subject to disaster, the disaster of the death of a sweet youth or the departure of a loved one?

Time and time again, the smiting down of youths and elders before my eyes affrights me, whether I abide at home or travel afar.

Sources: D i.254; M 41; H^1 92, H^2 81. Metre: *Ṭawīl*.

'A.JAA.ra/TA.NAA.laa.taj/ZA.^{c}*IY.wa/'A.NIY.biy*

'A.TAA.niy/MI.NAL.maw.til/MU.ṬIL.li/NA.ṢIY.biy

1. *muṭill* "nigh at hand" is applied to death with the implication that it may come on a man at any time. *'inābah* is a religious technical term for what in Western piety is called 'conversion'.

4. Excessive lamenting over a death is disapproved by Islam. Line 8 is based on the same idea.

12. See note on VII.19.

16. This presents, in a somewhat elaborate metaphor, a similar idea to that of line 12. The generations of men are pictured as parties of travellers starting out on life's journey at different times: the dead boy, in spite of having started later than his seniors, has reached the journey's end before them. In an added twist at the end, it is stressed that this was not of his own volition, but because he was driven on by an inexorable fate.

20. See note on VII.6.

XX

I was created with such qualities as I have, given no choice of my passion; had the choice been left to me, a clever fellow would I have been!

I desire, and am not given it; I am given when I did not desire; my wit is too small to fathom the secrets of providence.

I am turned away from my design, for all that my wit is so keen, and in the end I get as the outcome only amazement.

I sought to ride on fortune's back, in hopes that it might prove propitious, though it is so refractory a beast.

5 By my life, I have struggled, in spite of passion, to master my soul so that it may take comfort; but the yearning of my soul was too strong.

It is the strangeness of fate that to stand aside from it would be good counsel, and yet I have no power to stand aside.

Sources: D i.245-6; M 25; H^1 94, H^2 82. Metre: *Ṭawīl*.

K̲U.LIQ.tu/^{c}*A.LAA.maa.fiy/YA.ḠAY.ra/MU.K̲AY.ya.rin*

HA.WAA.ya/WA.LAW.k̲uy.yir/TU.KUN.tul/MU.HAD̲.d̲a.baa

4. The text given is that of M; *k̲aṭabtu* seems to have a generalized sense of "seek, desire" (rare, but recorded by Lane). The D ms. has (.)*aṭabtu* ^{c}*alā ḥabli*, the first letter being damaged; D edd. propose reading (*ḥ*) on the basis of a phrase *ḥaṭaba fī ḥablihim* "he gathered firewood in their rope" metaphorically used for "he acted in their interests", though it is questionable whether this idiom would permit the substitution of ^{c}*alā* for *fī*. If *ḥabl* is accepted, I would still read the verb with *k̲*- "I sought to be in control of fortune's rein".

XXI

If your brother is an oft-taster of passion, the steeds of his inclinations being turned in every direction,

then leave open for him the way of parting, and do not be the mount of a rider whose goings are all too frequent.

Your true friend is he who, when you give him cause for suspicion, says, 'It was I that did so'; and when you upbraid him, receives it mildly.

If you are inclined to reproach your friend over every matter, you will not find anyone whom you never have cause to reproach.

5 So live in solitude, or be in amity with your brother; sometimes he may avoid a fault, but sometimes cling to it.

If you do not at times drink a bitter cup and endure it, you must go thirsty; what man is there whose drink is always limpid?

Sources: D i.307; M 55; H^1 94, H^2 82. Metre: *Ṭawīl*.

'I.ḎAA.kaa/NA.ḎAW.waa.qan/'A.K̲UW.ka/MI.NAL.ha.waa

MU.WAJ.ja/HA.TAN.fiy.kul/LI.'AW.bin/RA.KAA.'i.buh

1. *ḏawwāq* is a term used in *Ḥadīṯ* for a philanderer, one who frequently changes his marital allegiance.

3. Authorities express two views about *'arāba*. Some say it is synonymous with *rāba*; others that *rāba* means to behave in such a way as to cause justified offense, while *'arāba* implies behaviour giving rise to suspicion not necessarily confirmed. If one here vocalizes *'arabta* or *'uribtu*, it is likely that the differentiated meaning is intended, so that the limiting force of *'innamā* falls on the verbal idea, 'your conduct may be suspicious but is not provenly wrong, and I will not believe mere suspicions'. But if one reads *'arabtu*, the limiting force probably falls on the pronoun, with the two verb forms used without differentiation of meaning: i.e. when a coolness arises, the true friend takes the blame on himself for being the offender.

5. At the beginning of the second hemistich the reading given is that of D, while M has *muqārifu* "yielding to"; with the M reading, *mujānib* will have to be understood in its other sense of "turning aside from".

6. It is interesting to see how far the phrase ^{c}*alā l-qaḏā* has become a dead metaphor, its original association with *'ig̲ḍā'* "winking one's eye" being virtually eliminated (compare the note on XVI.4).

XXII

The best of your two friends is he in whose society there is comfort and in whom, when he is far away, there is still advantage.

Intimacy belongs only to him who endears himself to you, even though a man may be born of Jurhum or Ṣudā'.

There is no good in a man who affects qualities he does not possess; true friendship is sincerity.

I will be reconciled with my friends, and pardon my close companion for any hasty deed he has incautiously committed;

how should I not pardon, even if he has vexed me, when my own soul is vexed by the deeds of my hands?

To reproach a man every day is a wretched business, and to set right the spites of women is a distress.

I can endure the greatest misfortune, but I cannot endure a company that disparages me.

I preserve my friendship by mildness, and in mildness have a cure for him possessed of the inveterate ill of rancour.

Sources: D i.128; H^1 95, H^2 83. Metre: *Ṭawīl.*

WA.K̲AY.ru/K̲A.LIY.lay.kal/LA.D̲IY.fiy/LI.QAA.'i.hiy

RA.WAA.ḥun/WA.FIY.hi.ḥiy/NA.ŠAṬ.ṭa/ḠA.NAA.'uw

2. Jurhum is the tribe which occupied Mecca before the arrival of Qurayš, and is often used to imply ancestry of immemorial nobility. At the end of the line the D ms. reads Ṣalā'u, by poetic license for Ṣalā'atu, a branch of the Qays ^{c}Aylān tribe; but since these had no special claims to fame, the D edd. propose reading Ṣudā'u, a Yemeni tribe elsewhere mentioned in connection with nobility.

XXIII

Time has swept away necklace and bangles, and my tears have flowed copiously for mortality.

I have lingered on for a day which is fast approaching, while my dear companions have already passed on in death.

My heart flutters like the wings of a bird, for tomorrow there is no escape from the bitter thing that is fate.

Among folk, if you know them well, is the man who is a king in receiving but a slave in giving,

one who makes demands of others, but bestows nothing on them; whose whole idea is 'give me this' and who has no notion of 'take this!'.

Often does a brother (apt to make a fine point) ask me about my two kinds of friend (they are not alike);

I reply, 'One is a pig, and the other a watchdog: the former is like most men, the latter gives tongue;

so choose the dog, with such qualities as he has — he will frighten away the thief and squat in the yard'.

Rare is the man whose forefathers are unblemished, and his mother-stock of fairest fame.

Become my intimate, and you will find me steadfast, a bosom confidant, honourable in brotherly love.

I never see you otherwise than wandering far and wide, labouring in travel to no purpose:

leave the world aside, and live in a shadowed corner of it, for the quest of worldly goods is a mortal disease.

Often to one that stays at home comes his daily bread, while the eager striver toils and yet is frustrated of his hope.

Man's perishing is one of his plagues: how hard to find would be one untouched by the wretchedness of perishing.

I see men regarding me as a lion, and they speak right and justly thus;

so be contented with the appointed lot bestowed by the Supreme Disposer, whereby a man may be destitute or become rich.

You who toil so anxiously to be assured of a sufficient livelihood, how trivial a thing is what suffices you after all your long toil.

Sources: D i.132; H^1 96, H^2 84. Metre: *Ramal*.

ḏa.HA.BAL.dah/ru.BI.SIM.ṭin/wa.BU.RAA

wa.JA.RAA.dam/ᶜi.YA.ṢAḤ.ḥan/fil.RA.DAA

1. The last word vocalized in D and H^1 as *ridā* = *ridā’* "on my coat"; H^2 does not vocalize it. In proposing the reading *radā* I suggest that the *’alif* at the end of the word is not significant, since mediaeval scribes pay very little attention to the 'classical' rules as to whether final *-ā* should be written with *’alif* or *yā*. 'Necklace and bracelets' for the D comm. means simply 'beauteous women', but for D edd. and H it is a metaphor for his friends who are the 'adornment' of his life.

11. *ḡanā* in H; the D text *ᶜanā* seems to be only a misprint.

15. *yarawnī* is for *yarawna-nī* (abbreviation in prose as well as verse). The 'lion' here probably refers to poetic superiority.

XXIV

O my two friends, trouble will surely find its cure, and ease may well follow on thereafter.

I am like time's drift itself: when it is unclouded, or when it is dull and overcast, I am the same.

O Admā', with my slender means I cannot run to silks and embroidery, and my little is good for nothing,

yet accept from my hand this modest offering. This age of ours is an unruly mount, and men's kindliness is slight.

5 I was formerly not content with a meagre livelihood, and no companion ever had cause to complain of niggardliness in me.

But, my two companions, wealth is of no advantage, since one cannot by it win a true brother or a trusty friend.

Formerly, when a place displeased me, I would take myself off to another wherein was no straitness for me.

As between God and man, no doer has ever been disappointed of his reward, who is possessed of a preeminence in piety or good works.

God's grace is not stinted from him who conducts himself uprightly; but it is men's natures that are mean-spirited.

Sources: A iii.240; M 247; H^1 97, H^2 85. Metre: *Tawīl*.

K̲A.LIY.lay/YA.'IN.nal.^{c}us/RA.SAW.fa/YU.FIY.quw

WA.'IN.na/YA.SAA.ran.fiy/ḠA.DIN.la/K̲A.LIY.quw

***

Lampoon and political pieces

The genre of *hijā'* perhaps corresponds rather to what we might call 'lampoon' than to the conventional rendering of the term as 'satire', for it is to a large extent caricature and pure and simple abuse. In the bedouin ambience, it was as much the poet's function to vilify his tribe's enemies as it was to sing the praises of his own tribe. In urbanized Muslim society, *hijā'* performed an equally important role as subserving political ends: poets were the political pamphleteers of the age. In addition, they often used *hijā'* to castigate their personal enemies, and to blackmail patrons into generosity if this did not come up to the poet's expectations. Needless to say, he was perfectly prepared to execute a complete volte-face of attitude should political or personal circumstances demand it.

XXV

Abū Ja^{c}far, length of life is not enduring; he who is now safe will soon be safe no more;

even upon the mighty king will destruction burst, and smite him down in the narrow strait of death.

You seem never to have heard of the death of a great crown-wearer, or of the annihilation of the Persians.

Chosroes was hewn asunder by the swords of his own folk, and Abū l-^{c}Abbās became a sleeper's dream,

even while he had no fear of the turning of any plot against him, nor the coming of ill-fated calamities,

but was constant in pleasures: until there appeared to him the faces of the Fates in unveiled horror.

The days ahead may come in lucky guise, or they may appear scowling, with all too manifest harshness.

Over Marwān's head did the millstone of war pass — and his crimes were petty to those which you have committed;

yet you still go purblindly on those men's way, and take no precautions against vengeances like those.

You have devoted yourself to Islam — but it was to efface its ways, and to leave its back bare to the fierce lions;

and you did not cease doing so, until Religion sought the aid of its adherents against you, and they put their trust in trenchant swords.

Seek as you may, son of Salāmah, a sure refuge to be your salvation, yet you will not escape from the oppressed when he turns oppressor.

God curse a folk who have made you their chief, when you have never ceased to be a slave to vile desires.

I will say to one who smiles, decked in magnificence, who has become a generous lover of noble deeds,

one of the descendants of Fāṭimah, who sound the clarion summons to Guidance (and who can guide you like the son of Fāṭimah?),

'You are a lamp for the eye of the seeker of light, but at another time darkness of death to the opposing foe'.

When the right course comes to the point of taking counsel, summon to aid the opinion of a faithful friend or the advice of a prudent man,

and reckon it no disgrace to seek counsel: for the underpinions are a strength to the forepinions.

What is the good of a hand bound to its fellow by the handcuff, and what is the good of a sword without the hilt's aid?

Leave 'Gently!' to the weakling; do not be a sluggard, for prudence is no sleeper.

Wage war, if you are given nothing but injustice: war's sting is better than meek acceptance of wrongdoing.

Admit to your intimacy one who brings himself close to you, but do not reveal your counsel to an man who cannot conceal it.

You will never expel cares by mere wishings, nor reach the heights otherwise than by noble deeds.

If you are one alone, folk will shun you as you come; if you are base, you will not win your ambitions.

No-one can smite the folk like a valiant man, well-disciplined; no-one can clear up blindness like a man of understanding.'

Sources: A iii.156; M 318; H^1 50, H^2 45. Metre: *Ṭawīl*.

'A.BAA.ja^{c}/FA.RIN.maa.ṭuw/LU.^{c}AY.šin/BI.DAA.'i.miy

WA.LAA.saa/LI.MUN.^{c}am.maa/QA.LIY.lin/BI.SAA.li.miy

This anti-Abbasid propaganda piece was composed in 145 A.H. at the height of the Alid revolt headed by Muḥammad known as al-Nafs al-Zakiyyah ("the Pure Soul"). After the collapse of the revolt, the poet is said to have redrafted it in order to remove the treasonable references, by substituting for Abū Ja^{c}far (the Caliph Manṣūr) and Salāmah (his mother), the names Abū Muslim (governor of Khorasan, who had fallen into disgrace and been put to death by Mansūr in 137 A.H.) and Wašīkah; and by suppressing line 15 with its references to the Fatimids.

1. ^{c}*ammā*, simply equivalent to ^{c}*an*, the *mā* being otiose (*zā'idah*).

2. *mutalāḥim* lit. 'with its sides pressing close on each other'.

4. Abū l-^{c}Abbās is the Caliph Ṣaffāḥ.

8. Marwān II, nicknamed 'the Ass', the last Umayyad Caliph.

14. The original allusion of this line must have been to Muḥammad 'the Pure Soul', but since the way he is described, and the advice tendered to him in the following lines, are all commonplaces, the passage was not dangerous to the poet after the collapse of the revolt.

25. Since the antithesis here is drawn between intellectual distinction and valour in war, *'adīb* can hardly refer to literary excellence but must have its original connotation of 'well-trained'.

XXVI

Is there a messenger, who will carry my message to all the Arabs,
to him among them who is alive and to him who lies hid in the dust?
To say, that I am a man of lineage, lofty above any other one of lineage:
the grandfather in whom I glory was Chosroes, and Sāsān was my father,
Caesar was my uncle, if you ever reckon my ancestry.
How many, how many a forebear I have, whose brow was encircled by his diadem,
haughty in his court, to whom knees were bowed,
coming in the morning to his court, clothed in blazing gems,
one splendidly attired in ermine, standing within the curtains,
the servitors hastening to him with golden vessels:
he was not given to drink the thin milk of a goatskin, or to sup it in leather vessels;
never did my father sing a camel-song, trailing along behind a scabby camel,
nor approach the colocynth, to pierce it for very hunger;
nor approach the mimosa, to beat down its fruits with a stave;
nor did we roast a skink, with its quivering tail,
nor did I dig for and eat the lizard of the stony ground;
nor did my father warm himself standing astraddle to the flame;
no, nor did my father use to ride the twin supports of a camel saddle.
We are kings, who have always been so through long ages past;
we brought the horsemen from Balkh, with no lie,
until we watered them (for we are not to be taken by surprise by the

enemy) in the twin streams of Aleppo;
then, when they had trampled on the hard earth of Syria,
we marched them to Egypt, in a noisy host,
so that we seized that realm, taking it into our realm that we had seized before;
and the horses brought us past Tangier, place of wonder,
so that we restored the sovereignty into the family of the Arabian Prophet.
Who is there that has fought against guidance and religion without being stripped?
Who, o who, has rebelled against it without being plundered?
For the sake of God and of Islam we are wrathful with a most noble wrath;
we are the possessors of crowns and of disdainful stiff-necked kingship.

Sources: D i.377; H^1 59, H^2 53. Metre: *Rajaz*.

hal.min.RA.SUW/lin.muḵ.BI.RIN

ᶜan.niy.JA.MIY/ᶜal.ᶜa.RA.BIY

This piece of anti-Arab and pro-Iranian propaganda contains a number of points which were stock arguments of the *šuᶜūbiyyah* party. Broadly, it divides into two parts: in the first, the glories of the long tradition of civilization among the Iranians are contrasted with the primitive barbarism of the Arab bedouin; second, the claim is made that the Iranians and not the Arabs are the true upholders of Islam, by having provided the principal force in the overthrow of the Umayyads, who are represented as irreligious enemies of Islam.

9. It was an ancient and widespread custom in the empires of the Near East for the sovereign to be veiled, behind a curtain, from the vulgar gaze.

11. The D comm. writes, '*siqan* is plural of *saqiyyah* and this is perhaps a noun meaning that which is given as drink'. This is not to be found in the lexica, and I suggest as more probable that the word is *siqā* = *siqā'*, a goat-skin container for milk or water. *'aqṭāb* is plural of *qaṭīb* "a mixed drink",

alluding to the fact that, when poor pasturage makes good milk scarce, it can be eked out by mixing with water or sour milk.

12. Camels are encouraged on the march by a chant of the rider or driver; the verb here has been wrongly printed in H[1,2] with *tanwīn* as if a noun.

13. The extremly bitter fruit of the colocynth (a gourd-like plant) was normally used in the ancient world medicinally; only under stress of famine could it be regarded as a foodstuff. The same applies to the mimosa of the next line.

15. The *waral* "skink" is a large lizard of the monitor type. Lizards were eaten and relished by the bedouin, a practice which their civilized neighbours regarded with disgust.

17. Bedouin wore a short kilt, above the knee; in this, to stand astraddle involves a risk of indecent exposure.

21. The D edd. point out that Aleppo has only one river, and conjecture that there may be a corruption; it is more likely that the dual is only a poetic license for metrical convenience.

24. D reads *istalamnā* "we received", but in favour of the H reading here adopted is the verbal echo it yields with *mustalab*.

25. As a matter of historic fact, the Abbasid armies never got further west than Barca. The D edd. therefore conjecture that the place here mentioned is not the well-known Tangier, but a locality cited by Yāqūt in his *Muᶜjam al-Buldān* as situated at Rās ᶜAyn in Egypt, where the Ayyubid al-Malik al-Ašraf had a palace and park. But it is very doubtful whether this existed in the time of Baššār, and it seems much more probable that this allusion is to what the Abbasids had hoped to do rather than to what they actually achieved. This also makes sense of the expression 'place of marvels', for there were several marvellous legends about the Straits of Gibraltar (e.g. that about the miraculous statue warning ships not to venture out into the Atlantic).

27. The questions in this and the next line are rhetorical, implying the answer 'nobody'. *lam yustalab* and *lam yuntahab* are circumstantial clauses (see Introduction).

XXVII

They sat down and chose for themselves a lineage which after nightfall might pass as Arab, but when morning came, it made plain the difference between their counterfeit coin and true gold:

men are now moneychangers well expert in basecoined lineage.

Sources: M 48; H[1] 62, H[2] 55. Metre: *Munsariḥ*.

hum.qa.ᶜA.DUW/fan.ta.QAW.LA/hum.ḥa.SA.BAN

yad.ku.LU.BAᶜ/dal.ᶜa.ŠAA.'I/fil.ᶜa.RA.BIY

Genealogies formed a favourite target for *hijā'*; specially since claims of Arab descent were often fictitious.

XXVIII

Treat ᶜAmr gently if you handle his genealogy, for he is an Arab of glass;

he has been constantly in a blacksmith's forge, which has turned him over and over until he has come out an Arab of most dusky tint

Sources: A iii.190; M 165; H[1] 62, H[2] 56. Metre: *Basīṭ*.

'ur.fuq.BI.ᶜAM/rin.'I.DAA/ḥar.rak.TA.NIS/ba.TA.HUW

fa.'in.NA.HUW/ᶜa.RA.BIY/yun.min.QA.WAA/riy.riy

1. The text is that of A; M is worded slightly (but not significantly) differently. The *qārūrah* is the small glass vessel, easily shattered, used by the barber-surgeon for the operation of blood-letting by the process of 'cupping'. Cp below XXIX.1 and XXX.9.

2. Ironical, and probably suggesting that he had negro blood in him.

XXIX

ᶜAmr, mark him well, is an Arab of glass,

of lineage so obscure you must take a candle to it to recognise it.

Sources: M 76; H[1] 63, H[2] 56. Metre: *Ramal*.

'in.NA.ᶜAM.ran/faᶜ.RI.FUW.huw

ᶜa.RA.BIY.yun/min.ZA.JAA.jiy

XXX

I have tested the Bani Zayd, and there are no traits of good sense among their elders, nor among their youngsters one who is decent.

Tell the Bani Zayd, and say to their chieftains (though in truth there are no chieftains among them worthy of reverence):

'Curses upon you; my odes are thunderbolts smiting highland and lowland alike'.

Can it really be that they do not shun baseness nor prefer the good (though good should be preferred)?

5 They gather the children of adultery into their numbers, so that their number exceeds that of all mankind!

Whenever they see one whose behaviour is like theirs, they flock round him, for folly always inclines to folly;

they have made a boast of those who resort to them in the evening; but I say, 'Boast on, if there is any cause for boasting in shame'.

They desire my eminence, but are further from attaining it than the sparkling lamps of heaven's gates are from earth.

Say of the Bani Zayd, as a gifted writer said, 'They are a cupper's glasses, which tomorrow will be shattered.'

Sources: A iii.204; M 159; H^1 58, H^2 52. Metre: *Ṭawīl*.

BA.LAW.tu/BA.NIY.zay.din/FA.MAA.fiy/KI.BAA.ri.him

ḤU.LUW.mun/WA.LAA.fil.'aṣ/Ḡ̣A.RIY.na/MU.ṬAH.ha.ruw

An accusation levelled against the Basran tribe of the Bani Zayd, on the grounds that they had unduly swelled their numbers by incorporating an excessive number of *mawālī*. The A explains that one of their chieftains complained to the poet that he had caused disaffection among their clients (probably by *šuᶜūbī* propaganda, cp XXVI), but was met with this rejoinder. In pre-Islamic times, sheer numerosity (*ᶜadad*) was one of the bedouin tribe's claims to distinction, along with good repute (*ḥasab*); but this became rather meaningless when the tribes began to accept vast numbers of non-Arabs as *mawālī*.

3. 'highlands and lowlands' apply metaphorically to all classes of the population.

4. *'a-jidda-hum* ... lit. "do they in all seriousness on their part do so-and-so?".

8. The stars are 'below', i.e. closer to the earth, than the possibility of their encountering (= gaining) my eminence. *masᶜāh* is behaviour by which glory is won.

XXXI

The comforting shade of prosperity is extended over ^{c}Abbās, yet his heart is forever fettered by miserliness.

A noble man conceals his destitution from you, that you may think him rich even when he is in difficulties,

but the miser, to protect his wealth, has excuses blue of eye and black of visage.

If you are reluctant to give even a small bounty, and cannot endure to be openhanded, there is no semblance of generosity in you.

Bring forth leaves of kindliness, so that you may be looked to for bounty; if the branch brings forth no leaves, one does not hope for fruit.

Scatter your bounty broadcast, and let its smallness not restrain you; every little thing that relieves poverty is praiseworthy.

Sources: A iii.195; D iii.127; M 100; H^1 58, H^2 52. Metre: *Basīṭ*.

ẓil.lul.YA.SAA/ri.^{c}A.LAL/^{c}ab.baa.SI.MAM/duw.duw

wa.qal.BU.HUW.'a.BA.DAN/fil.bak̲.LI.MA^{c}/quw.duw

The victim of this attack is the brother of the Caliph Manṣūr.

3. Blue eyes are generally regarded among the Arabs as unlucky and ill-omened. Blackness of face implies disgrace (cp Qur'ān iii.106).

XXXII

Seek not a man's spite which is more baneful than the pest; be circumspect and not rancorous in your imputations.

Why should I — weak as you are and without eminence — spare you while you invent unsparing lies?

Be careful! the pools of war are filled with deadly poison and bitter beneath the sweet.

At a time when you have bestowed your bounty on one who has uttered a single rhyme, while my verses are spread abroad in tribe after tribe,

have you now fastened your eye on us in a crooked glance of hatred? Had I placed my brand on you, your vision would have been no longer crooked.

Seek my good pleasure; seek not to embroil yourself with me: the feeble and decrepit cannot bear the loads I impose.

I am the earringed one; I am not hidden from anybody; the sun itself spreads my radiance to those near and far.

The Caliph in his splendour is like unto me: you are not like, so sleep, you vain foolish fellow.

The embassies wait, while I am summoned before their day of audience, for the royal gift; I come into the Caliph's presence by no magician's aid.

Were Yaḥyā a Tamīmī, I would maltreat him: but he is of Qurayš, a chick of the Baṭḥā';

Yaḥyā is a man of the Hashimites, fine is his stock, and not to be blamed, even if he was made to run with the sheep.

How noble is the man of Qurayš! we deny not his claim to kinship with the Prophet, even if he be the son of an ignoble mother;

his origin still lies in the heart of the Baṭḥā', though his ancestry be half papyrus, half rough hemp.

O lion of the tribe, when they return in the evening to a feast, but jackal of the tribe when they face the foe!

I have seared folk with my branding-iron, and they could not endure the torment, but have crept away with a grievous hurt.

Often has one who is closest to me gone too far in his words, but I have said to him (if he be of my folk or the offspring of my ancestors),

'Say what you will of falsehood and lies, my forbearance is deaf though my ear hears well'.

Sources: D i.122; M 5 (lines 2,5,17); H^1 63, H^2 56. Metre: *Basīṭ*.
laa.tab.ḠI.ŠAR/ram.RI.'IN/šar.ran.MI.NAL/daa.'iy
waq.daḥ.BI.ḤIL/min.WA.LAA/taq.daḥ.BI.ŠAḤ/naa.'iy

This is directed against another member of the Abbasid family, Yaḥyā b.Ṣāliḥ b.^{c}Alī b.^{c}Abd Allah b.^{c}Abbās. The theme is, 'Since you are a member of Qurayš, I will not vilify you in spite of your defects; but take warning and do not provoke me, for if I were to satirize you in earnest, I would crush you with shame'. The irony by which the uncomplimentary things said are claimed to be nothing compared with what might be said, is a common device of satirists.

4. The initial interrogative particle belongs with the main clause in the next line. Yaḥyā is represented as having hired a poet (though a very inferior one) to attack Baššār.

5. An allusion to the therapeutic use of cauterization. The 'brand' is the sting of Baššār's satire.

7. Mura^{cc}aṯ is said to have been a nickname of Baššār. The introduction to D (i.7) suggests that it may refer to a practice of women whose previous children have died to put earrings in a child's ears as a magical means of ensuring its living, or to a Persian practice of adorning valuable slaves with earrings. Neither suggestion accounts for the fact that the poet evidently took a pride in the name (since his own father was a slave, the second explanation seems specially unconvincing). A, however, contains (iii. 140) a story that he was so called because of affecting, instead of the style of shirt commonly worn, a special jacket style with high shoulder-pieces compared to earrings.

9. Foreign embassies were often kept waiting for long periods before being admitted to the sovereign's presence, in order to enhance the latter's dignity; it is here perhaps suggested that they might sometimes have resorted to magic in the hope of shortening the wait.

11. D vocalizes *'ajrā* , but this must be an inadvertence, for the note derives the word from *jrw* which in the 4th stem is applicable to a bitch, meaning "bring forth puppies"; hence a passive would be required, "even if he be whelped". I would prefer to take it from the much commoner root *jry*, also to be read in the passive, "be made to run". The reference to sheep alludes to the fact that herding was a despised occupation.

12. The D comm. makes *kallā'* the feminine of *kall* "an indigent person". But D edd., followed by H, identify it as one of the market places of Basra which was so called, thus implying that the object of the satire was 'a son of the market place', i.e. of vulgar descent. From the next line it appears that Yaḥyā's ancestry was half noble, half plebeian.

13. Baṭḥā' is the wadi running through Mecca. Papyrus is the antithesis of hemp because it was an expensive material.

14. An ironic inversion of the normal terms of praise: the true man should be in the forefront of the battle, but backward in the subsequent feasting; cp the *Lāmiyyah* of Šanfarā, line 8.

15. Cp note on line 5.

***

Eulogy

Eulogistic verse of the Muslim period is the most difficult of the peotic genres for modern European taste to appreciate. In the bedouin environment, bravery in battle and the generosity by which a man strips himself of his very livelihood in order to entertain the guest, were realities, the celebration of which carries conviction. But there is little reality about the endless and wildly hyperbolical catalogues of bravery and generosity with which Abbasid poets extolled inordinately wealthy noblemen who occasionally took part in the intermittent skirmishing on the Byzantine frontier. Such pieces were for the most part designed simply to extract money from the person praised, and the poet would as readily turn to satire if his piece failed to produce as big a dividend as he had hoped. In this direction, too, Baššār and his contemporaries had little scope for the sort of innovation displayed in other types of composition; the pieces had to please the patron, not the general public.Their appeal lies in untranslateable verbal artifice, in which the poets certainly displayed great virtuosity. The reader has to attune himself to the kind of rhetoric characteristic of English seventeenth and early eighteenth century verse.

XXXIII

A king to whom kings bow down, one who pays men full due, who sustains the Arabs;
observant of our reputations and honour, at all times a very Duwār or Nuṣub;
for whom dromedaries and mules do not cease to be laden with tribute rendered up unremittingly;
the hero of Qurayš for religion and magnanimity; to whom I have given my love in exchange for what he has given;
not purposing spite towards his friend, nor overmastered by rash deed when he is angered;
one who bestows his bounty on you as constantly as the winds blow; whose faith no-one can hope to shake, however close he be;
as a gruffly-growling lion you'll not find his equal, yet he is like water freshly flowing for one who would drink:
<u>to reach such a man's presence</u> I have assaulted the sandhills and

plains which separate him from me, urging on my highbred camels

made fit, on barley-mash and green fodder, for a pressing or overmastering business,

which tread on sand hot as embers of acacia-wood, when the mirage has begun to flicker and its intensity has veiled the dunes,

facing from every noontide a summer heat, and a flood that you can see boiling,

emaciated with travel, dropping their pace to a walk when the rider covers his face against the heat of the day,

or swimming through the rain-flood like the Adawlite vessel cleaving a sounding main,

until, when they had reached the tenting-place in the end, as guests of a protector who dissipates all cares,

I came in the morning at sunrise to him, whose hands rain gold on the visitors to his house.

When he saw me, his noble qualities appeared as a light on his face, and he was in no way cast down;

it was as if I had come to bring him good news, and had not come with greedy hope to milk his favour.

Mahdī has dissipated from me a stranglehold of painful cares which I had endured for many ages,

bestowing on me lavish wealth, slavegirls and slaves, until I fancied it was only a game for him,

scattering it broadcast to this one and that and that, making no reckoning, as another man would, of his bounty.

Surely he whose caliphate is of such benefit to mankind, that they struggle with each other for a way of access to him,

is the rival in glory of him by whom the prayer was established, who never committed an act of avarice nor told a lie:

with his qualities are Mahdī's dispositions intermingled, Mahdī has gor his inheritance of such from him, since to him does Mahdī trace his descent.

He goes forth in the morning with a blessing of prophetic grace, his thundercloud does not fail in its promise of rain when it is shaken by the thunder.

With Yūsuf al-Barm you made ready to fight, so that he tumbled headlong into hell.

The son of the pilgrims' waterer is sufficient guard for you against what may befall, both when he is at home and whatsoever beast he bestrides for a journey;

the Rightly-guided one of the people of prayer, concerning whom the priest chants an ancient scripture which has dispelled doubts.

He adorns the proud pulpit with his sides and his utterance when he preaches,

and the earth is refulgent with his excellencies, as though a borrowed light were added to the sun.

He is high in honour, one from whose hands the rain of bounty is sought, as his visitors resort to him in throngs;

he is the final objective of the delegations when they journey, hoping with eager desire for his bounty,

the night-traveller among them saying, when they have toiled on their journey, 'When morning comes there will be rejoicing for him who has toiled'.

When you come to Mahdī, to ask of him, you will meet in him with both generosity and merit;

on him you may see the mark of the Prophet; and if he wars against a folk he kindles for them a burning flame.

But peace has shone forth under his rule; of him says one who can read the scriptures,

'Muḥammad bequeaths his succession to Moses and Aaron, for them to follow a father's pattern in him'.

Sources: D i.326; M 26 (lines 17,28); H^1 53, H^2 47. Metre: *Munsariḥ*.

wa.ma.LI.KUN/tas.ju.DUL.MU/luw/ku.LA.HUW

muw.fin/^{c}*A.LAL/naa.si.YAR.ZU/qul.*^{c}*a.RA.BAA*

Addressed to the Caliph Mahdī, this is an extract from a much longer poem, in the most formal style of eulogy.

1. The D vocalization *malikin* (implying the *wa* which means *rubba*) is, as the D comm. points out, erroneous; it would be highly inappropriate in this

context, where the whole point is that Mahdī was unique. What one has to understand is "he is a king ...".

2. Duwār and Nuṣub were idols reverenced by the pagan Arabs.

6. In early Arabic, *ṭamaʿa fī* often means not simply "aspire to" but "entertain hostile intentions towards". I am sceptical about the D edd. interpretation of *mā habbat il-riyāḥu* as "wherever the winds blow" (making the verb transitive with its object an implied pronoun referring back to *mā* envisaged as relative); the interpretation of *mā* as "so long as" seems much more natural, with the verb intransitive.

9. The D edd. propose emending *muʿaddāt* to *mugaḏḏāt* "nourished". *lajīn* is leaves mixed with barley, used as camel fodder.

11. I am inclined to think that *ḥabab* "bubbles" alludes to the effect of mirage making the air seem like boiling water; though one could, in the light of line 13, suppose a real flood to be meant.

12. *ʿūj* "crooked", because a camel's hump falls in as a result of travel exhaustion, instead of being firm and rigid.

13. *ʿadrah* "heavy rain" is recorded in the *Munjid*, though rather surprisingly it has been omitted by Lane. *ʿadawliyy* is a derivative from the place-name Adulis, a shipbuilding port on the western coast of the Red Sea.

17. *muḥtaliban* is the reading of M and A. The D ms. reading is uncertain, but the printed text has *muḵtaliban* "snatching".

22. *šaqīq* is the D ms. reading; the D edd. emend this to *samiyy* on the grounds that it is impossible to call Mahdī 'brother' of 'him by whom the prayer was established', i.e. the Prophet. Presumably they mean their emendation to be taken in the sense of "namesake" (Mahdī's personal name was Muḥammad), since the other sense of this word, "rival, compeer" would be just as hyperbolical as *šaqīq*. But in view of the subsequent lines in the piece, it does not seem beyond the bounds of possibility that Baššār may here have indulged in this admittedly rather extreme hyperbole.

23. A not untypical example of the extreme freedom of Arabic in the matter of ambiguities of pronoun reference; it is left to the hearer to sort out which of the pronouns refers to Mahdī and which to the Prophet.

Mahdī, by virtue of being a member of the Prophet's family, has inherited the Prophet's qualities.

25. Yūsuf al-Barm raised a revolt against Mahdī in Khorasan in 160 A.H.
26. 'The pilgrims' waterer': ^{c}Abbās b.^{c}Abd al-Muṭṭalib, progenitor of the Abbasids, had the function (the *siqāyah*) of providing water for pilgrims.
27. The 'people of prayer' are the Muslims, and the rest of the line alludes to the Muslim tenet that the Scriptures, if read aright, foretell Islam. The accusative pronoun in *yaqra'u-hū* is odd, and here seems to stand for *fī-hi* "concerning whom".
31. *wufūd* is an allusion to this technical term of the beginnings of Islam, when the 'missions' from the bedouin tribes came to the Prophet to give their allegiance to Islam, for which they received rewards.
32. The metre requires *sarī-himū/ī*.
36. In this line, Muḥammad is Mahdī himself. The idea expressed is that, whereas normally a man emulates the great deeds of his predecessors, Mahdī is so superior to Moses and Aaron as to reverse the normal order of things, and give them more cause to emulate him and follow his example, as if he had been their predecessor instead of the other way round.

XXXIV

By my life, Ibn Barmak has been generous to me, though not everyone who has riches is generous.

I have milked by my verses his two palms, and they have streamed with bounty as do the clouds in thunder weather.

If you come to him with praise, his face shines upon you and he will bestow on you munificence in exchange for praise.

His are favours bestowed on folk, for which he asks in return no recompense or tradesman's measure, pound for pound.

Beneficent is he, and spendthrift; the manner of his wealth, when he goes out at morning or returns at night, is like the ocean's ebb and flow.

K̲ālid, praise endures as a glory for one who deserves it; but worldly treasures do not endure in spite of all one's pains:

so feed the hungry, and eat of your possessions as if of a loan due to be repaid; spare not, for loans are made only for recall.

Sources: A iii.192; D iii.125; M 115; H^1 52, H^2 47. Metre: Ṭawīl.

LA.^{c}AM.riy/LA.QAD.'aj.daa/^{c}A.LAY.yab/NU.BAR.ma.kiy

WA.MAA.kul/LU.MAN.kaa.nal/ḠI.NAA.^{c}in/DA.HUW.yuj.diy

Addressed to the famous vizier Ḵālid al-Barmakī.

5. The D edd. make *sabīl* accusative, "he is spendthrift as to the manner of dealing with his wealth"; the A make it nominative, and punctuate after *mitlāfun*. The latter to my mind gives a better reading of the line. However, the A edd. also propose to emend *turāṯ* (read by D ms. and edd., as also M) to *ṯarā'*, on the grounds that *turāṯ* means 'what a man bequeaths to his heirs' which they say is inappropriate here; but in fact there is little doubt that the word is also used in the sense (appropriate here) of "what a man inherits as heir". The simile can, I think, be interpreted in two ways. Either 'ebb and flow' together mean simply 'the ocean', i.e. his bounty is as boundless as the ocean. Or there is a rhetorical point in the two words: his wealth in the evening is like the flood tide, but in the morning like the ebb — because by then he has spent it all on his guests of the previous evening. Cp a line of ᶜUrwah b.al-Ward, "Night brings to me the guests of a noble generous man, but my flocks, when they go out to pasture in the morning, are those of a poor man" (having been slaughtered to provide the entertainment).

XXXV

I have drunk muddied lees of wine, but had the pools of Sulaymān been near, limpid would have been my drink.

When you come to Harran and visit its prince, your watering will be assured and your valley lush,

for there dwells a man with ready gift for him who draws near, a man who has a welcoming abode and a hand yielding milk,

a hand that gives abundantly of life to a folk at his good plasure, though it is death to them when he is angered.

You who seek to be befriended by fortune, you whom tooth and talon of distress and wretchedness have touched!

if Fate's eye is bleared, then cure it by drawing near to Sulaymān, and you shall be comforted;

enmity shall pass you by, so long as marshals in full armour, gray haired seniors, march beneath his banners.

He is the true man, who exalts Qurayš by his aid and his repelling of a wicked enemy when he rages;

weighty in skill of learning, he is not swayed by tales to which the faultfinder would give ear.

He is like the Caliph himself, and by his sword is fear inspired in times of stress, and it is to his sword that all rally.

His heart leaps at the moment of the holy war; dyed fingertips touch him not;

when war stirs, he stirs in order to reduce it again to quiescence, even while the turmoil of the troops is at its height.

Every year he raids with an embattled host, his plan bringing death in its train when he goes forth —

a mighty army, in whose packed masses the swords seem like stars of the sky, as the light flashes back and forth between them;

vast numbers of cavalry cease not making incursions whereby Byzantium's monarch is sore vexed and troubled;

the daughters of Leo, after his return, being shared out as booty among the fellow-soldiers, seemed does –

donatives, for which he who wins them is envied, choicest of the captives of Byzantium, virgins and matrons.

Never did his cavalry strike at an outlaw folk and turn away from anything save weltering blood;

when he goes out in the morning to war, he is likely to leave mourning women, with keening and lament over the slain.

Splendid is he, with lance like that of Hišām; when he traces his ancestry, he was bred of sires like full moons, among which is no paltry star;

fair of countenance when he goes, as though picked out among men, placed in the very forefront of praise.

He decks with grace the throne of kingship, and by him is made resplendent the pulpit set up on the day when he delivers the homily.

Sources: D i.130; H^1 77, H^2 68. Metre: *Ṭawīl*.

ŠA.RIB.tu/BI.RAN.qin.min/MU.DAA.min/WA.LAW.da.nat

ḤI.YAA.ḍu/SU.LAY.maa.nin/ṢA.FAA.li/YA.MAŠ.ra.buw

Addressed to the Umayyad prince Sulaymān b.Hišām b.ᶜAbd al-Malik in Harran.

2. The second-person pronouns are vocalized in both editions as feminine, explained as being addressed to the poet's she-camel.

3. The D ms. reading *'inna l-nawāla* — syntactically almost impossible to construe; hence the D edd. propose emending to *dānī l-nawāli*. *sahl* (lit. "smooth") is intended to evoke the normal greeting form *'ahlan wa-sahlan*. *ᶜaṭan* is properly a "stable", but often used for the dwelling of someone to whom travellers resort.

11. Dyed fingertips implies women, who stain their fingers with henna. For *yataṭarraq* H reads *yataṭarrab* "delight". According to the D comm., the *jazm* form of the imperfect is a poetic license, not implying the prohibitive use of *lā*. However, the D edd. suggest emending *lā* to *lam*, thus avoiding any anomaly.

12. *yuᶜīdu* is the D edd. emendation for ms. *yufīdu*, which is an awkward expression, because although peace is an advantage to men, it is not so to war, which is normally represented as rejoicing in its destructive activities. It seems to me that *ḥuṯḥūṯ* is the *maṣdar* of *ḥaṯḥaṯa* "put into a state of commontion", and this fits fairly easily with *muṭnib*, which is known in the sense of "going to an extreme". But both the D edd. and H take *ḥuṯḥūṯi l-katībati* in a concrete sense, "large body of troops".

13. An allusion to the early Islamic practice of staging regular summer raids on Byzantine territory.

16. *'alyūn* is the emperor Leo III "the Isaurian", 99-123 A.H./717-40 A.D. (not Leo IV, son of Constantine, as H's note wrongly has). The D comm. takes *ṣaḥā'ib* as an irregular plural of *ṣāḥibah* "fellow female (prisoners)", but the D edd. as a plural of a plural, from *ṣaḥābah* the collective of *ṣāḥib*.

18. *muḥill* is (see Lane) a person whom it is lawful to slay, the antithesis of *muḥrim*.

20. Hišām, Umayyad caliph, father of Sulaymān.

XXXVI

One of Mālik's race, before whose face war gives way as does the gloom before a light.

You who question me as to prudence and valour, boldness, bounty and good faith:

these are the qualities possessed by Ibn Salm, and even more than equals those in beneficence.

Like the outpourings of heaven is the generosity of his hands, both to a kinsman and to one whose home is far off, distant.

God forbid that you should see the like of Ibn Salm, good ^{c}Uqbah, nourisher of the poor.

The birds swoop down where grain is scattered, and the dwellings of the noble are a resort for men.

He gives to you not for hope or fear, but simply that he delights in the taste of giving.

The delight of Ibn Salm, the liberal, is solely in giving, and in a battle-steed;

he does not fear the din or war, nor is he a slave to money, rather he despises it for the sake of praise;

generous, having one hand which rains bounty, and another which is deadly poison to enemies.

He has clothed me in silk, and made houris to serve me, and decked my dear daughter in bridal array,

and freely bestowed on me that slave most splendid, long of arm, smooth of cheek, fresh in manliness

— but God decreed that he should die, as our sons and our fathers before us have died:

he departed borne on his bier, and I betook myself to ^{c}Uqbah with my tale of woe, and he spoke out clearly:

'If one servitor has been smitten down, I have ready another servant like him',

and I obtained him straightway, a proud one like the lion's whelp which comes upon you as he issues from the forest;

so may God reward Ibn Salm on behalf of your brother - at a time when kindliness is rare - with the best of rewards.

His hands have cherished me so that I seem to be wealthy, among truly wealthy folk.

I care nothing for rejection by the mean man, nor do my tears flow over any traitor to sincerity;

but ^{c}Uqbah purchases glory by praiseworthy deeds, and looks on blame as a thing vile as the spotted serpent.

He is a king who ascends the pulpits in virtue, but on the day of bloodshed he pours out blood.

How many a benefit he has to bestow on us and among us, and kindly deeds towards the worthy.

He is a lion who crunches up men, yet many a time he is a thunderous raincloud, a copious downpour from the sky;

one who bears the banner aloft, who would protect the Caliph's sanctity against mankind at the price of his own death.

Salute to ^{c}Uqbah at all times, whether he be at home or journeying under the shadow of the martial banner.

Sources: D i.110; H^1 79, H^2 70; a few lines in A.iii.189,194, and M 7.

Metre: *K̲afīf*.

maa.LI.KIY.yun/tan.SAQ.QU.^{c}an/waj.HI.HIL.ḥar

bu.KA.MAAN.saq/qa.TIL.DU.jaa/^{c}an.ḌI.YAA.'iy

Addressed to ^{c}Uqbah b.Salm b.Qutaybah, governor of Basra under Manṣūr.

8. ^{c}Uqbah rejoices in being sought out by petitioners.

11. Text and interpretation according to H. D has the rather obscure *k̲allā ... fī l-k̲ulā'i*.

12. *bi-hī*, the pronoun is allusive to a slave-boy whose qualities are then described. This and the following lines are criticized by the D comm. as falling into bathos: the poet's slave is a triviality not worthy of mention in the catalogue of ^{c}Uqbah's glories; or at least, though the gift might be mentioned as an instance of the patron's generosity, it is inappropriate to expatiate on a slave's excellencies.

17. 'Your brother' is the poet himself; 'your' being a vague address to the hearer.

18. *ṣana^{c}at* evokes the usage of *ṣanī^{c}ah* in the sense of a person taken under a patron's protection, a 'creature' of the patron (though without the disparaging connotations of the English usage). It should be borne in mind that *sirr* does not invariably mean "secret", but often implies what is 'real' and not merely superficial.

21. For *faḍl* the D edd. suggest possibly reading *faṣl* "eloquence".

22. *'in ši'ta*, see note to VII.6.

XXXVII

Greatly loved has Sulaymān become; around him we revolve as do the Arabs around the *qiblah*-house.

You see him clothed with splendour by virtue of his ancestors, with magnificence by virtue of his own hand which is dewy with liberality and is stripped of its possessions by giving.

Excellence shows forth plainly to you in him when you look on him, as it does in the smile of a full-bosomed maiden with pearly teeth.

Sword, and lance, and valorous ancestors of his, have raised Sulaymān to an exalted eminence.

Ah, how fortunate is one who has occupied his place among them, and drunk of the water which they drank;

firmly established was their kingship (there is no faith but the sword), victorious their days from the most ancient past;

the lives of a folk may sometimes be prolonged at their hands but sometimes, when they are angry, may be cut short untimely,

while they tie knots of death, in the midst of a picked host, whose vanguard is driven on by a pounding gallop:

they are keen swords and noble paladins, dolour and destruction come upon him who does battle with them.

I say to one who girds against a fate which illtreats him, a fate involving ignominy, gap-toothed like a lion,

'There is none to compare with Sulaymān and his family as protector against the enemy, or against an unlucky fate;

when you meet Abū Ayyūb, whether he be at home or on campaign with the banners waving over him,

you meet the rolling waves of a lake which is not diminished by the drinking of those who wade into its borders:

so drink with enjoyment, and rank yourselves among his adherents, and prosper - the peaceful life of the prosperous is the only true delight'.

Ibn Dā'ūd the Hashimite has solaced us, though he owes us nothing by way of kindliness or kinship;

he has restored to us life, so that its fresh shoots wave in the wind, and has befriended us so that all cares are removed from us through him.

He is a lion in war, kindling or dowsing its flame as he wills; and you will never see the like of what he gives and bestows;

harsh at times, but at times we find him mild; over him is the canopy of kingship and behind him the clamorous host.

The pilgrim's waterer was his worthy ancestor (well did the nobles of Qurayš know) and his were the standards and lance-pennants to be followed,

who brought to Ḥunayn his swords and a noble steed with tangled forelocks, made slender by being trace-led and set to gallop;

giving his lifeblood in defence of God's Prophet, so that he wore it as a glorious mantle, while his sword was stained with it.

Dā'ūd was a great mountain, whereby one could shade oneself; in ᶜAlī lay rout for the enemies of truth.

Virtue belongs to Ibn ᶜAbbās; great deeds in the cause of religion are reckoned to him, and pious conduct.

Say to anyone who seeks to rival in glory Sulaymān and his family, 'Alas, supple willow is in no way like sturdy oak:

destine your father for other deeds than his, and acknowledge that there is a folk having a summit that overtops the tangled undergrowth'.

These are sons of the rulers over all who pray to our *qiblah*, and each one of them is a king whose brow is encircled by the diadem.

The blood of the Prophet is infused into their blood, as thick honey mingling with water of the raincloud.

Had any folk before them been given mastery over the sun, *these* would have ruled over both the sun by day and the full-moon by night, and no lie!

God has bestowed on them what He bestowed on no other; they are kings, riding out to meet the enemies of prudent counsels.

They care not for wealth, with its incitement to miserliness, for it is the vile who care for their riches.

Were it not for Sulaymān's excellencies and benevolence, a man who seeks for righteous dealing would never know whence its branches spring.

When fate is unpropitious, to him resort constantly both the kinsman who can claim his protection and the stranger looking for a windfall;

how many an orphan there is, with downcast gaze, having no resource except to partake of bounty at the hands of the wealthy man,

for whom Sulaymān provides what would be the mainstay of a rich man, and thereby he comes away in the evening as would another man whose kinship is linked to Sulaymān,

with a lavish gift, not accompanied by any pride of giving (though other folks take credit for their virtue and reckon it unto themselves).

Son of parents noble in ancestors and mighty deeds! from you comes fulfilment and the wished-for gift.

In the tribe I have a brood of children, with matted hair, for whom I am troubled; children who cannot earn, while I possess no competence for them;

rarely do they get a bite of food after their one meal a day - how must you feel, towards human beings whose livelihood is but a single meal?

Sources: D i.233; H^1 81, H^2 71. Metre: *Basīṭ*.

'am.saa.SU.LAY/maa.NU.MAR/'uw.man.NU.ṬIY/fu.BI.HIY

ka.maa.TU.ṬIY/fu.BI.BAY/til.qib.LA.TIL/ʿa.RA.BUW

Addressed to Sulaymān b.Dā'ūd b.ʿAlī b.ʿAbd Allah b.ʿAbbās, a cousin of Manṣūr.

6. The adjective derived from the name of the ancient South Arabian tribe of ʿĀd is often used to describe something of great antiquity and distinction. *ḡulub* is for *ḡulb*, plural of *'aḡlab*.

7. The prolongation of life is by generosity; there is the usual rhetorical parallelism between bountifulness in peace and valour in war (cp.XXXV.7).

8. *musawwamah* "marked" implies marked by special insignia for recognition in battle. The D ms. has *tuzjā 'awā'iluhā*, which is difficult; the reading given here is the emendation of the D edd.

9. *yuʿādī* in the D ms., though the edd., followed by H, propose reading *tuʿādī* "with whom they do battle".

10. *šuʿab* are gaps between the teeth, a feature said to be characteristic of the lion.

12. Cp XXXVI.25.

15. Obligation is incurred either by the mere fact of mutual clan membership or by benefits (*ni^{c}mah*) calling for repayment, but his generosity is exercised when there is no obligation of either kind.

18. The reading given is that of the D edd. and H, with *mirāran* balancing *tārātin*; the D ms. has *ṣa^{c}ban mazāran* "difficult of access", which the edd. think incompatible with eulogy. However, it could be suggested that it is intended to glorify his kingly remoteness (also hinted at in the second part of the line, and on which see note to XXXII.9), and that the word has its rhetorical balance in *nuwāfiquhū*. To say that a canopy and an army are both 'over' (*^{c}alā*) him would be virtually impossible in English, but is not so in Arabic, where it is normal to speak of guards, servants &c. who stand(in English terminology)'behind' someone, as standing 'over' him.

19. See note on XXXIII.26.

20. *muqrabah*, a mare of special excellence kept close to her owner's tent. Ḥunayn is the famous battle of 8 A.H.

21. *irtadā zaynahā* lit. "he mantled himself in the adornment of his own blood".

24. The two tree names are used in poetry and proverb to signify contrasting qualities. The *nab^{c}ah* is a tree growing in the mountains, with a particularly dense and hard wood, so that 'oak' furnishes an English parallel.

25. The 'folk' here are Sulaymān's family, compared to a mountain top rising conspicuous above overgrown lower slopes.

27. Cp XXXIII.23.

31. *^{c}urf* stands for the more usual *ma^{c}rūf* "approved conduct". *yanša^{c}ibu* is glossed by H (with a query) as *yaḏhabu*, by the D edd. as *yanṣaliḥu* "be set to rights, be in good order". Both suggestions seem rather feeble. I would conjecture that the poet had in mind the expression *inša^{c}abat 'aḡṣānu l-sajarati* "the boughs of the tree branched out", with the implication that Sulaymān's virtue is as it were the main trunk from which other instances of virtue are only secondary branchings-out.

32. *kabā* "stumble", fate being compared to an untrustworthy mount that stumbles and throws its rider. The *'aqrab* and the *junub* are the two classes of those who can look to a tribal chieftain for assistance; the former

claims it by right of kinship, the latter is a non-member of the clan who claims it from the chieftain's generosity.

33. *'ašab* is claimed by the D comm. as a synonym of *kasab* "means of livelihood", but this is not recorded in the classical lexica. H, more convincingly, sees in it a metaphor (typical of bedouin language) whereby the basic meaning "tangled vegetation" implies lushness and rich living.

34. *'āḵā* is not the *fāᶜala* stem (meaning "adopt as a brother") but probably, as Lane suggests, an *'afᶜala* stem; the sense being "provide someone with something he needs". *nāla rawāḥa 'āḵara* lit., "obtains the coming-away-in-the-evening of another man".

35. The original sense of *sabiṭ* "long" is linked to that of lavishness by the concept that a generous man has 'a long arm'. *mann* here, as not uncommonly, is to be taken not in the simple sense of "conferring a benefit" but that of taking an ostentatious pride in so doing.

(١)

قالوا بمن لا ترى تهذى؟ فقلت لهم   الأذن كالعين توفى القلب ما كانا
ما كنت أوّل مشغوفٍ بجارية   يَلقى بلقيانها رَوحًا وريحانا
يا قوم أذنى لبعض الحىّ عاشقة   والأذن تعشق قبل العين أحيانا

(٢)

لم يطل ليلى ولكن لم أنم   ونفَى عنّى الكرى طيفٌ ألَمّ
وإذا قلت لها جُودى لنا   خرجَتْ بالصمت عن لا ونعم
رفّهى يا عبد عنّى واعلمى   أننى يا عبد من لحم ودم
إنّ فى بُردِىَ جسمًا ناحلا   لو توكّأتِ عليه لانهدم
ختم الحبّ لها فى عنقى   موضع الخاتم من أهل الذمم

(٣)

عبد إنّى قد اعترفت بذنبى   فاغفرى واعركى خطاى بجنبى
عبد لا صبرَ لى ولست، فمهلا،   قائلا قد عتبتِ فى غير عتب
ولقد قلت حين أنصبنى الحبّ   فأبلَى جسمى وعذّب قلبى
ربِّ لا صبر لى على الهجر حَسْبى   فأقِلْنى حسبى لك الحمد حسبى

(٤)

يا عبد زورينى تكن منّةً   لله عندى يومَ ألقاك
والله ثمّ والله فاستيقنى   أنّى لأرجوك وأخشاك
يا عبد إنّى هالك مدنف   إن لم أذق برد ثناياك
فلا تردّى عاشقا مدنفا   يرضى بهذا القدر من ذاك

(٥)

يا ليلتى تزداد نكرا   من حبّ من أحببت بكرا
حوراء إن نظرَتْ اليـ   ـك سقتك بالعينين خمرا
وكأنّ رجع حديثها   قِطَعُ الرياض كُسِينَ زهرا
وكأنّ تحت لسانها   هاروت ينفث فيه سحرا
وتخال ما جمعَتْ عليـ   ـه ثيابَها ذهبًا وعطرا
وكأنّها برد الشرا   ب صفا ووافق منك فطرا
جنّيّة إنسيّة   أو بين ذاك أجَلُّ أمرا
وكفاك أنّى لم أُحِط   بشكاة من أحببتُ خبرا
إلّا مقالة زائرٍ   نثرت لِىَ الأحزان نثرا
متخشّعًا تحت الهوى   عشرا وتحت الموت عشرا

(٦)

يا صاحبَيَّ العشيّةَ ٱحتسبا   جدَّ الهوى بالفتى وما لعبا
واللهِ والله ما أنامُ ولا   أملك عينى دموعها طربا
أبقَى لنا الدهرُ من تذكُّر من   قد كان جارا فبان واغتربا
لله دمعِى ألّا أُكلّمَه   يوم غدا فى السلاف منشعبا
ما كان ذنبى أنّى شُقيت به   وشؤمُ عينٍ كانت لنا سببا
أفرغتُ دمعى على الحبيب فأعـ   ـجبت رجالا ولم أكن عجبا
قبلى تصابى الفتى ومال به   حبّ المعاصير عفّ أو خلبا
ما كان حبّى سلمَى ورؤيتها   إلا قذًى فى مدامعى نشبا
أُريد نسيانها فيذكّرنى   ما بات فى الجارتين مكتسبا
لله سلمى إذ لا تطيع بنا الـ   ـواشى وإذ لا نطيع من عتبا
تدنو مع الذكر كلّما نزحت   حتى أرى شخصها وما اقتربا
ويومَ أشكو الى أسامة مكـ   ـنون الهوى فاستطار والتهبا
قالت سُلَيمَى أعندنا شغل   عنك ولكن لا تُحسِن الحلبا
أكرِمْ خليطا تَنَلْ كرامته   لست بجانٍ من شوكه عنبا
زينَ الجوارى خُلِقتِ من عجب   والحرص عجلانُ يفضح الأدبا
وبالنقَى والعيونُ حاضرة   عيّـنّنا كلَّ شارق عُقَبا
دسّت الىّ البنانَ تخبرنى   عنها فمَنَّى وربما كذبا
كانت على ذاك ثَمّتِ آنقلبت   كما دعوتُ الزماع فانقلبا
كم من نعيم نلنا لذاذته   ومجلسٍ عاد ذكرُه نصبا
لم يبق إلا الخيال يذكرنى   ما كان منها وكان مطّلبا
دَعْ عنكَ سلمى شجًى لطالبها   لا يسبق الرأى دون ما كُتبا
سأترك الغرّ للعيون ولا   أترك شرب الصهباء والغربا

(٧)

لقد زادنى ما تعلمين صبابةً   اليكِ فللقلب الحزين وجيب
وما تُذكَرين الدهرَ إلا تهلّلَتْ   لعينىّ من شوق اليكِ غروب
أَبيتُ وعينى بالدموع رهينة   وأُصبح صبًّا والفؤادُ كئيب
إذا نطق القوم الجلوس فإنّنى   مكبّ كأنّى فى الجموع غريب
يقولون داء القلب جِنّ أصابه   ودائى غزال فى الحجال ربيب
إذا شئتُ هاج الشوقَ واقتاده الهوى
اليك من الريح الجنوب هبوب

هوى صاحبى ريحُ الشمال إذا جرت　　وأهوى لقلبى أن تهبّ جنوب
وما ذاك إلا أنّها حين تنتهى　　تَناهَى وفيها من عبيدة طيب
وإنّى لمستشفى عبيدة ــ إنّها　　بدائى وإن كاتمتُه لطبيب
كقارورة العطّار أو زاد نَعْتُها　　تلين إذا عاتبتها وتطيب
لقد شغلتْ قلبى عبيدةُ فى الهوى　　فليس لأخرى فى الفؤاد نصيب
ألا تتّقين الله فى قتل عاشق　　له حين يمسى زفرة ونحيب
يقطّع من أهل القرابة ودّه　　فليس له إلا هواك نسيب
تمنّيننى حسن القضاء بعيدةً　　وتلويننى دَينى وأنت قريب
فوالله ما أدرى أتجحد حبّنا　　عبيدة أم تجزى به فتثيب
وإنّى لأشقَى الناس إن كان حبّها　　خصيبا ومرتاد الجناب جديب
وقائلةٍ إن متّ فى طلب الصبا　　فلا بدّ أن تُحصَى عليك ذنوب
فرُمْ توبة قبل الممات فإنّنى　　أخاف عليك الله حين تؤوب
تَكلّفُ إرشادى وقد شاب مفرقى　　وحمّلنى أهلى فليس أُريب
فقلت لها لم أَجْنِ فى الحبّ بيننا　　إثامًا على نفس فممّ أتوب ؟
أرانا قريبا فى الجوار ونلتقى　　مرارا ولا نخلو وذاك عجيب
ألا ليت شعرى هل أزورك مرّة　　وليس علينا يا عبيد رقيب
فنشفى فؤادينا من الشوق والهوى　　فإنّ الذى يشفى المحبّ حبيب
وما أنسَ ممّا أحدث الدهر للفتى　　وأيّامه اللائى عليه تنوب
فلست بناسٍ من رضابك مشربا　　وقد حان من شمس النهار غروب
فبتّ لما زوّدتِنى وكأنّنى　　من الأهل والمال التلاد حريب
إذا قلت يُنسِينيك تغميضُ ساعةٍ　　تعرّض أهوال لكم وكروب

(٨)

أيها الساقيان صُبّا شرابى　　وآسقيانى من ريق بيضاء رود
إنّ دائى الظما وإنّ دوائى　　شربة من رضاب ثغرٍ بَرود
ولها مضحك كغُرّ الأقاحى　　وحديث كالوشى وشى البُرود
نزلت فى السواد من حَبّة القلب　　ونالت زيادة المستزيد
ثمّ قالت نلقاك بعد ليالٍ　　والليالى يُبلين كلّ جديد
عندها الصبر عن لقائى وعندى　　زفرات يأكلن قلب الحديد

(٩)

إذا لاح الصوار ذكرت سلمى　　وأذكرها إذا نفح الصوار
كأنّك لم تزر غُرّ الثنايا　　ولم تجمع هواك بهنّ دار

يروّعه السِرار بكلّ شيء　　مخافةَ أن يكون به السرار
كأنّ فؤاده كرة تنزّى　　حذارَ البين لو نفع الحذار
أقول وليلتى تزداد طولا　　أما للّيل بعدهم نهار
كأنّ جفونه سُمِلت بشوك　　فليس لنومه فيها قرار
جفتْ عينى عن التغميض حتّى　　كأنّ جفونها عنها قصار

(١٠)

طال ليلى من حبّ من　　لا أراه مقاربى
أبدًا ما بدا لعيـ　　ـنك ضوء الكواكب
أو تغنّت قصيدةً　　قينةٌ عند شارب
فتعزّيت عن عبيـ　　ـدة والحبّ غالبى
تلك لو بيع حبّها ابـ　　ـتعته بالحرائب
ولَوِ آستطعت طائعًا　　فى الامور النوائب
لفداها من الرَدَى　　هاربى بعد قاربى
عتبت خِلّتى وذو الحـ　　ـبّ جمّ المعاتب
من حديث نمى اليـ　　ـها به قولُ كاذب
فتقلّبتُ ساهرًا　　مقشعرّ الذوائب
عجبا من صدودها　　والهوى ذو عجائب
ولقد قلت والدمو　　ع لباسُ الترائب
لو بدا اليأس من عبيـ　　ـدة قد قام نادبى
عبد بالله أطلقى　　من عذاب مواصب
رجلا كان قبلكم　　راهبا أو كراهب
يسهر الليلَ كلّه　　نظرًا فى العواقب
فثناه عن العبا　　دة وجدٌ بكاعب
شغلته بحبّها　　عن حساب المحاسب
عاشق ليس قلبه　　من هواها بتائب
يشتكى من فؤاده　　مثلَ لسع العقارب
وكذاك المحبّ يلـ　　ـقى بذكر الحبائب
ولقد خفت أن يرو　　ح بنعشى أقاربى
عاجلا قبل أن أرى　　فيكمُ لين جانب
فإذا ما سمعتِ با　　كيةً من قرائبى
ندبتْ فى المسلّبا　　ت قتيلَ الكواعب

فاعلمى أنّ حبكّم … قادنى للمعاطب

(١١)

ريق سعدى يابن الدجيل الشفاء … فاسقنيه لكلّ داء دواء
نام عنّى صحبى ولا أعرف النو … م بعينى قذى وبالقلب داء
ويقول الوشاة أحببتَ سعدى … صدقوا والجليلِ حبّى عياء
لا أرانى أعيش قد ظعن الحِبّ … وحقّت بيوتى الاعـــداء
ذهب الناصح الشفيق وأمسى … جارَ بيتى البغيضُ هذا البلاء
جاورتـنا كالماء حينًا فلمّا … فارقت لم يكن لحرّان ماء
فصِلِ الليل بالنهار الى أحْوَ … ر فيه تعرّض والتِـواء
واسترِحْ بالحبيب فيما تلاقى … كلّ شىء سوى الحبيب عناء
ويقول الطبيب فى رحمة اللـــــــه غناءٌ وليس عندى غناء
أمَمٌ ما سلمت فَقْدُ فقيد … أىّ نفس صفا لها ما تشاء ؟
ليس يبلى بالصبر عنه وفى طو … ل زمان يأتى عليك عزاء
نُصُب الحادثات غير سليم … كلّ كأس له بـــها أقذاء

(١٢)

خشّاب، هل لمحبّ عندكم فرج … أو لا ؟ فإنّى بحبل الموت معتلج
لو كان ما بى بخلق الله كلّهم … لا يخلصون الى أحبابهم درجوا
للهجر نار على قلبى وفى كبدى … إذا نأيت ورِيا وجهك الثلج
كأنّ حبّك فوقى حينَ أكتمه … وتحت رجلىّ لجّ فوقه لجج
قد بُحْتُ بالحبّ ضيقًا عن جلالته … وأنت كالصاع تُطوى تحته السُرُج
خشّاب، جودى جهارا أو مسارقةً … فقد بليتُ ومرّت بالمنى حِجج
حتّى متى أنت يا خشّاب جالسة … لا تخرجين لنا يوما ولا نَلِج ؟
لو كنت تلقين ما نلقى قسمت لنا … يوما نعيش به منكم ونبتهج
لا خير فى العيش إن كنّا كذا أبدًا … لا نلتقى وسبيلُ الملتقى نهج
من راقب الناس لم يظفر بحاجته … وفاز بالطيّبات الفاتق اللهج
وقد نهاك أُناسٌ لا صفا لَهُمُ … عيشٌ ولا عدموا خصمًا ولا فلجوا
قالوا حرام تلاقينا، فقد كذبوا، … ما فى التزام ولا فى قبلة حرج
أما شعُرْتِ، فَدَتْكِ النفس جاريةً، … أن ليس لى دون ما منّيتنى فرج
إنّى أبشّر نفسى كلّما اختلجت … عينى أقول بنيل منك تختلج
وقد تمنّيتُ أن ألقاك خاليةً … يوما، وأنّى وفيما قلت لى عوج ؟
أشكو الى الله شوقًا لا يفرّطنى … وشُرّعا فى سواد القلب تختلج

يا ربِّ لا صَبْرَ لى عن قرب جارية   تـنأى دلالًا وفيها إن دنَتْ غنج
غرّاءَ حوراءَ من طيبٍ إذا نكهت   للبيت والدار من أنفاسها أرج
كأنّها قمر رابٍ روافــــــدُه   عذبِ الثنايا بدا فى عينه دعج

(١٣)

سلّمْ على الدار بذى تنضب   فشطّ حوضى فلوى قعنب
واستوقفِ الركبَ على رسمها   بل حُلّ بالرسم ولا تركب
وصاحبٍ قد جُنّ فى صحّة   لا يشرب التِرياق من عقرب
جافٍ عن البيض إذا ما غدا   لم يبك فى دار ولم يطرب
صاديتُه عن مُرّ أخلاقِـه   بحلو أخلاقى ولم أشغـب
حتّى إذا ألقى علينا الهوى   أظفارَه وارتاح فى الملعب
أصفيته ودّى وحــدّثته   بالحقّ عن سعدى وعن زينب
أقول، والعين بها غـصّةً   من عبرة هاجت ولم تسكب،
إن تذهب الدار وسكّانها   فإنّ ما في القلب لم يذهب
لا غَرْوَ إلّا دار سكّاننا   تمشى بها الرُبْد مع الربرب
تنتابها سعدى وأترابـها   فى ظلّ عيش حافل معجب
مرّ علينا زمنٌ مصعب   بعد زمان ليس بالمصعب
فاجتـدّ سعدى بحذافيرها   غير بقايا حبّها المصحب
قد قلت للسائل فى حبّها   لـمّا دنا فى حرمة الأقرب
يا صاحِ لا تسأل بحبّى لها   وانظر الى جسمِيَ ثمّ اْعجب
من ناحلِ الألواحِ لو كِلْتَه،   فى قلبها مَرّ ولم ينشب
أغرى بسعدى عندنا فى الكرى   من ليس بالدانى ولا المصقب
مـكّية تبدو إذا ما بدت   بالميث من نعمان أو مغرب
عُلِّقتُ منها حُـلُمًا كاذبا   يا ليت ذاك الحلم لم يكذب

(١٤)

لعبدة دار ما تكلّمنا الدار   تلوح مغانيها كما لاح أسطار
أُسائل أحجارا ونؤْيا مهدّما   وكيف يجيب القولَ نؤى وأحجار؟
وما كلّمتنى دارها إذ سألتها   وفى كبدى كالنفط شُبّت به النار
وعند مغانى دارها لو تكلّمت   لمكتئبٍ بادى الصبابة أخبار

(١٥)

يا منظرا حسنا رأيته   من وجه جارية فديته
بعثتْ الىّ تسومنى   بُردَ الشباب وقد طويته

والله ربّ محمد   ما إن غدرتُ ولا نويته
أمسكتُ عنكِ وربّما   عَرَضَ البلاءُ وما ابتغيته
إنّ الخليفة قد أبى   وإذا أبى شيئا أبيته
ومخضّبٍ رخص البنا   ن بكى علىّ وما بكيته
ويشوقنى بيت الحبيـ   ـب إذا ادّكرت، وأين بيته ؟
قام الخليفة دونه   فصبرت عنه وما قليته
ونهانى الملك الهُما   م عن النسيب وما عصيته

(١٦)

والله لولا رضا الخليفة ما   أعطيت ضيما علىّ فى شجن
وربّما خِيرَ لابن آدم فى الـ   ـكره وشقّ الهوى على البدن
فاشرب على أُبنة الزمان فما   تلقى زمانا صفا من الأُبَن
الله يعطيك من فواضله   والمرء يغضى عينا على الكُمن
قد عِشْتُ بين الريحان والراح والـ   ـمزهر فى ظلّ مجلس حسن
وقد ملأتُ البلاد ما بين فغـ   ـفور الى القيروان فاليمن
شعرًا تصلّى له العواتق والـ   ـشيب صلاةَ الغواة للوثن
ثمّ نهانى المهدىّ فانصرفتْ   نفسى صنيعَ الموفّق اللقن
فالحمد لله لا شريكَ له   ليس بباقٍ شىءٌ على الزمن

(١٧)

قد لامنى فى خليلتى عمرُ   واللوم فى غير كنهه ضجر
قال أَفِقْ قلت لا فقال بلَى   قد شاع فى الناس عنكما الخبر
فقلت إن شاع ما اعتذارِىَ مـ   ـمّا ليس لى فيه عندهم عذر ؟
لا أكتم الناسَ حبَّ قاتلتى   لا لا ولا، أكره الذى ذكروا
لُوما فلا لَوْمَ بعدها أبدًا   صاحبُكم والجليلِ محتضر
قم قم اليهم فقل لهم قد أبى   وقال لا لا أُفيق فانتحروا
ما ذا عسى أن يقول قائلهم   وذا هوى ساق حينَه القدر؟
يا قوم ما لى وما لهم أبدا ؟   ينظر فى عيب غيره البطر
يا عجبًا للخلاف يا عجبا   بفى الذى لام فى الهوى الحجر
ما لام فى ذى مودّة أحدٌ   يؤمن بالله قم فقد كفروا
حسبى وحسب التى كلِفتُ بها   منّى ومنها الحديثُ والنظر
أو قُبلة فى خلال ذاك ولا   بأسَ إذا لم تُحلَّل الأزر
أو لمس ما تحت مرطها بيدى   والباب قد حال دونه الستر

أو عضّة فى ذراعها ولها   فوق ذراعى من عضّها أثر
والساق بـرّاقة خلاخلُها   والصوت عالٍ فقد علا البهر
واسترخَتِ الـكفّ للغزال وقا   لت أُلْهُ عنّى والدمعَ منحدر
اذهب فما أنت كالذى ذكروا   أنت وربّى مُعارِك أشِـر
وغابت اليوم عنك حاضنتى   فالله لى اليوم منك منتصر
يا ربّ خذ لى فقد ترى ضعفى   من فاسق الكـفّ ما به سكر
أهوَى الى معضدى فرضّضه   ذو قـوّة ما يُطاق مقـتدر
يُلصِق بى لحيةً له خشنت   ذات سواد كأنّـهـا الإبر
حتّى علانى وأُسْرتى غيب   وَيْلِى عليهم، لو انّهم حضروا
أقسم بالله ما نـجوتَ بها   اذهب فأنت المساور الظفر
كيف بأمّى إذا رأت شفتى   أم كيف إن شاع منك ذا الخبر؟
أم كيف لا كيف لى بحاضنتى   يا حَبَّ لو كان ينفع الحذر
قد كنت أخشى الذى ابتُلِيتُ به   منك فما ذا أقول يا عبر؟
قلت لها عند ذاك يا سكنى   لا بأس إنّى مخرّب خبِـر
قُولى لهم بـقّة لها ظُفُرٌ   إن كان فى البقّ ما له ظفر

(١٨)

إنّما عظم سليمى حبّتى   قصب السكّر لا عظم الجمل
وإذا أدنيت منها بصلا   غلب المسك على ريح البصل

(١٩)

أجارتنا لا تجزعى وأنيبى   أتانى من الموت المطلّ نصيبى
بنيّـىعلى رغمى وسخطى رُزِئْتُهُ   وبُدِّل أحجارا وجالَ قليب
كأنّى غريب بعد موت محمّد   وما الموت فينا بعده بغريب
صبرت على خير الفتـوّ رزئته   ولولا اتّقاء الله طال نحيبى
لعمرى لقد دافعتُ موتَ محمّد   لو انّ المنايا ترعوى لطبيب
وما جَزَعى من زائلٍ عمَّ فَجْعُه   ومن وردِ آبارى وقصد شعيبى؟
فأصبحت أبدى للعيون تجلّدا   ويا لك من قلب عليه كـئيب
ولى كلَّ يوم عبرةٌ لا أفيضها   لأَحْظَى بصبر أو بحـطّ ذنوب
دعَتْه المنايا فاستجاب لصوتها   فلله من داعٍ دعا ومجيب
أظلّ لأحداث المنون مروّعا   كأنّ فؤادى فى جناح طلوب
عجبت لإسراع المنيّة نحوه   وما كان لو مُلّيتُه بعجـيب
رُزئت بنيّـى حين أورق عوده   وألقى علىّ الهمّ كلّ قريـب

وقد كـنت أرجو أن يكون محمّد   لنا كافيا من فارس وخطيب
وكان كريحان العروس بقاؤه   ذَوَى بعد إشراق يسرّ وطيب
أغرّ طويل الساعدين سميذع   كسيف المحامى هُزّ غير كذوب
غدا سَلَف منّا وهجّر رائحٌ   على أثَر الغادين قَوْدَ جنيب
وما نحن إلّا كالخليط الذى مضى   فرائس دهرٍ مـخطئٍ ومصيب
نـؤمّل عيشا فى حياة ذميمة   أضـرّت بأبدان لنا وقلـوب
وما خيرُ عيشٍ لا يزال مفـجّعا   بموت نعيم أو فراق حبيب ؟
إذا شئت راعتنى مقيما وظاعنا   مصارعُ شبّانٍ لدىّ وشيب

(٢٠)

خلقت على ما فىّ غير مخيّـر   هواى ولو خيّرت كـنت المهذّبا
أريد فلا أُعطَى وأعطى ولم أرد   وقصّر علمى أن أنالَ المغيّـبا
وأُصَرف عن قصدى وعلمِىَ ثاقبٌ   فأرجع ما أعقبت إلّا التعـجّبا
خطبت على ظهر الزمان لعلّه   يساعفنى يوما وإن كان أنكبا
لَعمرى لقد غالبتُ نفسى على الهوى   لِتَسْلَى فكانت شهوة النفس أغلبا
ومن عجبِ الأيّام أنّ اجتنابها   رشاد وأنّى لا أطيق التجنّبا

(٢١)

إذا كان ذوّاقا أخوك من الهوى   موجّهة فى كلّ أوب ركائبه
فخَلِّ له وجهَ الفراق ولا تكن   مطـيّةَ رحّال كثير مذاهبه
أخوك الذى إن ربتَه قال إنّما   أربت وإن عاتبته لانَ جانبه
إذا كـنتَ فى كلّ الأمور معاتبا   صديقَك لم تلق الذى لا تعاتبه
فعِشْ واحدا أو صِلْ أخاك فإنّه   مفارق ذنب مـرّةً ومجانبه
إذا أنت لم تشرب مرارا على القذى   ظمئت، وأىّ الناس تصفو مشاربه؟

(٢٢)

وخير خليليك الذى فى لقائه   رواح وفيه حين شطّ غناء
وما القرب إلّا للمقـرِّب نفسَه   ولو ولدتْه جرهمٌ وصداء
ولا خيرَ فى ودّ امرئٍ متصنّعٍ   بما ليس فيه والوِداد صفاء
سأُعتِب خلّانى وأعذر صاحبى   بما غلبته النفس والغُلَواء
وما لِىَ لا أعفو وإن كان سائنى   ونفسى بما تجنى يداى تساء؟
عتاب الفتى فى كلّ يوم بلـيّة   وتقويم أضغان النساء عناء
صبرت على الجُلَّى ولست بصابر   على مجلس فيه علىّ زراء
وإنّى لأستبقى بـحلمى مودّتى   وعندى لذى الداء الملحّ دواء

(٢٣)

ذهب الدهر بسمط وبرا   وجرى دمعِىَ سحًّا فى الردا
وتأيّيت ليوم لاحق   ومضى فى الموت إخوان الصفا
ففؤادى كجناحَىْ طائرٍ   من غد لا بدّ من مُرّ القضا
ومن القوم إذا ناسمتهم   ملك فى الأخذ عبد فى العطا
يسأل الناس ولا يعطيهم   هَمُّه "هاتِ" ولم يشعر بـ"ها"
وأخٍ ذى نيقة يسألنى   عن خليلىّ، وليسا بسوا
قلت خنزيرٌ وكلب حارس   ذاك كالناس وهذا ذو ندا
فخُذِ الكلب على ما عنده   يُرعب اللصّ ويقعى فى الفنا
قلّ مَن طاب له آباؤه   وعلى أمّاته حسن الثنا
اُدْنُ منّى تلقنى ذا مِرّة   ناصح الجيب كريما فى الإخا
ما أراك الدهرَ إلّا شاخصا   دائب الرحلة فى غير غَنا
فدَعِ الدنيا وعِش فى ظلّها   طلبُ الدنيا من الداء العَيا
ربّما جاء مقيما رزقُه   وسعى ساعٍ وأخطا فى الرجا
وفَناء المرء من آفاته   قلّ من يسلم من عِيِّ الفنا
وأرى الناس يرونى أسدا   فيقولون بقصد وهدا
فارْضَ بالقسمة من قسّامها   يعدم المرء ويغدو ذا ثرا
أيّها العانى ليُكفَى رزقَه   هانَ ما يكفيك من طول العنا

(٢٤)

خليلىّ إنّ العسر سوف يفيق   وإنّ يسارا فى غد لخليق
وما كنتُ إلّا كالزمان إذا صحا   صحوت وإن ماق الزمان أموق
أأدماءُ لا أسطيع فى قلّة الثرى   خزوزا ووشْيًا والقليلُ محيق
خُذى من يدى ما قلّ، إنّ زماننا   شموس ومعروف الرجال رقيق
لقد كنت لا أرضى بأدنى معيشة   ولا يشتكى بخلا علىّ رفيق
خليلىّ إنّ المال ليس بنافع   إذا لم يُنَل منه أخ وصديق
وكنت، إذا ضاقت علىّ محلّة   تيمّمتُ أخرى ما علىّ تضيق
وما خاب بين الله والناس عاملٌ   له فى التُقَى أو فى المحامد سوق
ولا ضاق فضل الله عن متعفّف   ولكنّ أخلاق الرجال تضيق

(٢٥)

أبا جعفر ما طول عيش بدائم   ولا سالم عمّا قليل بسالم
على الملك الجبّار يقتحم الرَدى   ويصرعه فى المأزق المتلاحم

كأنّك لم تسمع بقتل متوّج   عظيم ولم تسمع بفتْك الأعاجم
تقسّم كسرى رهطُه بسيوفهم   وأمسى أبو العبّاس أحلامَ نائم
وقد كان لا يخشى انقلابَ مكيدة   عليه ولا جَرْىَ النحوس الأشائم
مقيما على اللذات حتّى بدت له   وجوه المنايا حاسرات العمائم
وقد تَرِدُ الأيّام غــرّا وربّما   وردن كُلوحًا باديات الشكائم
ومروان قد دارت على رأسه الرحى   وكان لما أجرمتَ نَزْرَ الجرائم
فأصبحتَ تجرى سادرا فى طريقهم   ولا تـتّقى أشباهَ تلك النقائم
تجرّدت للإسلام تعفو سبيلَه   وتُعرِى مطاه لليوث الضراغم
فما زلت حتّى استنصر الدينُ أهلَه   عليك فعاذوا بالسيوف الصوارم
فرُم وَزَرًا ينجيك يا ابن سلامة   فلست بناجٍ من مضيمٍ وضائم
لحا الله قوما رأّسوك عليهمِ   وما زلت مرؤوسا خبيثَ المطاعم
أقول لبسّام عليه جلالة   غدا أريحيّا عاشقا للمكارم
من الفاطميين الدعاة الى الهدى   جهارا ، ومن يهديك مثل ابن فاطم؟
سراجٌ لعين المستضىء وتارةً   يكون ظلاما للعدوّ المزاحم
إذا بلغ الرأىُ المشورةَ فاستعِنْ   برأى نصيحٍ أو نصيحة حازم
ولا تجعل الشورى عليك غضاضةً   فإنّ الخوافى قوّة للقوادم
وما خيرُ كفٍّ أمسك الغلّ أختَها   وما خير سيف لم يؤيَّد بقائم ؟
وخَلِّ الهوينا للضعيف ولا تكن   نــؤوما فإنّ الحزم ليس بنائم
وحارِبْ إذا لم تُعْطَ إلّا ظلامة   شبا الحربِ خيرٌ من قبول المظالم
وأدنِ من القربى المقرِّبَ نفسَه   ولا تُشهد الشورى آمرءًا غير كاتم
فإنّك لن تستطرد الهمّ بالمُنى   ولن تبلغ العليا بغير المكارم
إذا كنت فردا هرّك القومُ مقبلا   وإن كنت أدنَى لم تفرّ بالعزائم
وما قرع الأقوامَ مثلُ مشيّع   أديب ولا جلّى العَمَى مثلُ عالم

(٢٦)

هل من رسول مــخبر   عــنّى جميع العرب
من كان حيّا منــهمُ   ومن ثَـوَى فى الترب
بأنّنى ذو حسب   عالٍ على ذى الحسب
جَدّى الذى أسمو به   كسرى وساسانُ أبى
وقيصرٌ خالى إذا   عددتَ يوما نسبى
كم لى وكم لى من أب   بتاجه معــتصب
أَشْوَسَ فى مجلسه   يُجْثَى له بالرُّكَب

يغدو الى مجلسه　　فى الجوهر الملتهب
مستفضل فى فَنَكٍ　　وقائم فى الحجب
يسعى الهبانيق له　　بآنيات الذهب
لم يسق أقطاب سقا　　يشربها فى العلب
ولا حدا قطّ أبى　　خلفَ بعير أجرب
ولا أتى حنظلة　　يثقبها من سغب
ولا أتى عرفطة　　يخبطها بالخشب
ولا شوينا وَرَلًا　　منضنضا بالذنب
ولا تقصّعتُ ولا　　أكلت ضبّ الحزب
ولا اصطلى قطّ أبى　　مفحّجا للهب
كلّا ولا كان أبى　　يركب شرجَىّ قطب
إنّا ملوك لم نزل　　فى سالفات الحقب
نحن جلبنا الخيل من　　بلخ بغير الكذب
حتّى سقيناها - وما　　نُبْدِهُ - نهرَىْ حلب
حتّى إذا ما دوّخت　　بالشام أرض الصلب
سرنا الى مصر بها　　فى جحفل ذى لجب
حتّى استلبنا ملكها　　بمُلكنا المستلب
وجازت الخيلُ بنا　　طنجةَ ذات العجب
حتّى رددنا المُلك فى　　أهل النبىّ العربى
من ذا الذى عادى الهدى　　والدينَ لم يستلب ؟
ومن ومن عانده　　أو جار لم ينتهب ؟
نغضب لله ولـ　　ـلإسلام أسرَى الغضب
نحن ذوو التيجان والـ　　ـمُلك الأشمّ الأغلب

(٢٧)

هم قعدوا فانتقوا لهم حسبا　　يدخل بعد العشاء فى العرب
حتّى إذا ما الصباح لاح لهم　　بيّن ستّوقهم من الذهب
والناس قد أصبحوا صيارفةً　　أعلم شىءٍ بزائف الحسب

(٢٨)

أرفق بعمرو إذا حرّكت نسبته　　فإنّه عربىّ من قوارير
ما زال فى كير حدّاد يردّده　　حتّى بدا عربيًّا مظلم النور

(٢٩)

إنّ عمرا فاعرفوه عربىّ من زجاج
مظلم النسبة لا يعـــــــرف إلّا بالسراج

(٣٠)

بلوت بنى زيد فما فى كبارهم حلوم ولا فى الأصغرين مطهّر
فأبلغْ بنى زيد وقل لسراتهم وإن لم يكن فيهم سراة توقّر
لأمّكم الويلات إنّ قصائدى صواعقُ منها مُنْجِدٌ ومغوّر
أَجَدَّهم لا يتّقون دنيّة ولا يؤثرون الخير والخير يؤثر ؟
يلفّون أولادَ الزنا فى عدادهم فعِدّتهم من عِدّة الناس أكثر
إذا ما رأوا مَن دأبُه مثل دأبهم أطافوا به والغىّ للغىّ أصْوَر
لقد فخروا بالملحقين عشيّة فقلت افخروا إن كان فى اللوم مفخر
يريدون مسعاتى ودون لقائها قناديلُ أبوابِ السماوات تزهر
فقُل فى بنى زيد كما قال مُعرب قواريرُ حجّام غدًا تتكسّر

(٣١)

ظلّ اليسار على العبّاس ممدود وقلبه أبدا فى البخل معقود
إنّ الكريم لَيخفى عنك عسرته حتّى تراه غنيّا وهو مجهود
وللبخيل على أمواله عِللٌ زرق العيون عليها أوجه سود
إذا تكرّهتَ أن تعطى القليلَ ولم
تقدر على سعة لم يظهر الجود
أورِقْ بخير تُرجَّى للنوال فما ترجى الثمارُ إذا لم يورق العود
بُثَّ النوالَ ولا تمنعْك قلّته فكلّ ما سدّ فقرًا فهو محمود

(٣٢)

لا تبغ شرّ امرئ شرّا من الداء واقدحِ بحلم ولا تقدح بشحناء
ما لى وأنت ضعيف غير مرتقب أبقى عليك وتفرى غير إبقاء ؟
مهلًا فإنّ حياض الحرب مُترعة من الذعاف مِرارٌ تحت حلواء
أحينَ طُلتَ على من قال قافية وطال شعرى بحىّ بعد أحياء
ألزمتَ عينك من بغضائنا حَوَلًا لو قد وسمتك عادت غير حولاء
أطلبْ رضاى ولا تطلبْ مشاغبتى لا يحمل الضَرِع المقورّ أعبائى
أنا المرعّث لا أخفى على أحد ذرّت بىَ الشمس للدانى وللنائى
يغدو الخليفة مثلى فى محاسنه ولستَ مثلى فنَمْ يا ماضغ الماء
يثوى الوفود وأُدعَى قبل يومهمِ الى الحباء ولم أحضر برقّاء

لو كان يحيى تميميّا أسأتُ به   لكنّه قرشىّ فَرْخُ بطحاء
يحيى فتًى هاشمىّ عزّ جانبُه   فلا يُلام وإن أُجرِى مع الشاء
نِعْمَ الفتى من قريش لا ندافعه   عن النبىّ وإن كان ابن كلّاء
ما زال فى سُرّة البطحاء منبتُه   مقابلا بين بردىّ وحلفاء
يا أسد الحىّ إن راحوا لمأدبة   وثعلب الحىّ إن ذافوا لأعداء
كويتُ قوما بمكواتى فما صبروا   على العقاب وقد دبّوا بدهياء
وربّما أغرق الأدنى فقلت له،   إن كان من نَفَرى أو نَجْلَ آبائى،
قل ما بدا لك من زور ومن كذب   حلمى أصمّ وأذنى غير صمّاء

(٣٣)

وملك تسجد الملوك له   موف، على الناس يرزق العربا
راعٍ لأحسابنا وذمّتنا   يمسى دوارا ويغتدى نصبا
لا تفتر البُخْتُ والبغال موا   قيرَ خراجًا يُحبَى له دأبا
فتى قريش دينا ومكرمةً   وهبتُ ودّى له بما وهبا
لا يأثر الغِلَّ للخليل ولا   تغلبه طيرة إذا غضبا
يعطيك ما هبّت الرياحُ ولا   يُطمَع فى دينه وإن قربا
يكفيك من قَسْوَر أجشّ وكالـ   ـماء زلالًا يجرى لمن شربا
ساورتُ من دونه العقنقل والـ   ـجوف أُزجى المهريّة النجبا
من المعدّات فى اللجين وفى الـ   ـعيس لهمٍّ ألحّ أو غلبا
يخبطن جمر الغضا وقد خفق الآ
ل وغشّى ريعانُه الحدبا
مستقبلات من كلّ هاجرة   قيظا وفيضا ترى له حببا
عُوجً توالَى على الذميل إذا   الراكب من حَرّ يومه انتقبا
يسبحن فى عَدرة السماء كما   شقّ العدولىّ زاخرًا صخبا
حتّى إذا خيّمتْ بعاقبة   جاراتِ والٍ يفرّج الكربا
صبّحتُه فى الذرور تمطر كفّـ   ـاه لزوّار بيته ذهبا
لمّا رآنى بدت مكارمُه   نورا على وجهه وما اكتأبا
كأنّما جئتُه أبشّره   ولم أجئ راغبا ومحتلبا
فرّج عنّى المهدىّ من كُرَب الضيـ   ـق خناقا قاسيته حقبا
أعطى من الصتم والولائد والـ   ـعبدان حتّى حسبتُه لعبا
يحثى لهذا وذا وذاك ولا   يحسب معروفه كمن حسبا
إنّ الذى أنعمتْ خلافتُه   بالناس حتّى تنازعوا سببا

شقيقُ من قامت الصلاة به   لم يأت بخلًا ولم يقل كذبا
شيبت بأخلاقه خلائقه   وحاز ميراثَه إذا انتسبا
يغدو بيُمْنٍ من النبوّة لا   يُخلِف عرّاصُه إذا اضطربا
ويوسف البرم قد عبأتَ له   حتّى هوى فى الجحيم منقلبا
إنّ ابن ساقى الحجيج يكفيك ما حلّ   مقيما وأيّــــةً ركبا
مهدىّ آل الصلاة يقرؤه الــقسّ   كتابا دَثْرا جلا ريبا
يزيّن المنبر الأشمّ بعطــفَيه   وأقواله إذا خطبا
وتشرق الأرض من محاسنه   كأنّ نورا فى الشمس مجتلبا
أغرّ مستمطر اليدين إذا   راح عليه زوّارُه عُصبا
ومنتهى غاية الوفود إذا   ساروا يرجّون وصله رغبا
يقول ساريهم وقد دأبوا   بعد الصباح اغتباطُ مَن دأبا
إذا أتيتَ المهدىّ تسأله   لاقيتَ جودًا به ومحتسبا
ترى عليه سيما النبىّ وإن   حارب قوما أذكى لهم لهبا
قد سطع الأمنُ فى ولايته   وقال فيه من يقرأ الكتبا
محمّد مُورِثٌ خلافتَه   موسى وهارون يتبعان أبا

(٣٤)

لعمرى لقد أجدى علىّ ابن برمك   وما كلّ من كان الغنى عنده يجدى
حلبت بشعرى راحتيه فدرّتا   سماحًا كما درّ السحاب مع الرعد
إذا جئته للحمد أشرق وجهُه   اليك وأعطاك الكرامة بالحمد
له نِعَمٌ فى القوم لا يستثيبها   جزاءً وكيلَ التاجر المدَّ بالمدّ
مفيدٌ ومتلافٌ سبيلُ تراثه   إذا ما غدا أو راح كالجزر والمدّ
أخالدُ إنّ الحمد يبقى لأهله   جمالا ولا تبقى الكنوز على الكدّ
فأَطعِمْ وكُلْ من عارة مستردّة   ولا تُبقِها إنّ العوارى للردّ

(٣٥)

شربت برنق من مدام ولو دنت   حياض سليمان صفا لى مشرب
إذا جئتِ حرّانا وزُرتِ أميرها   فريُّكِ مضمون وواديك مشعب
هناك امرؤٌ دانى النوال لمن دنا   له عطنٌ سهل وكفٌّ تحلّب
دَرور لقوم بالحياة على الرضى   على أنّ فيها موتَهم حين يغضب
ألا أيّها المستعتب الدهر مسّه   من الضيق والتأنيب نابٌ ومخلب
إذا قَذِيَت عينُ الزمان فداوِها   بقرب سليمان فإنّك معتب
عداكَ العِدى ما سار تحت لوائه   بطاريق فى الماذىّ كهل وأشيب

هو المرء يستعلى قريشا بنفعه ودفع عدوٍّ فاحش حين يكلب
رزينُ حصاةِ العلمِ لا يستخفّه أحاديثُ يستوعى عليها المعيّب
شبيهُ أمير المؤمنين وسيفُه به يُتّقَى فى النائبات ويُعصب
يهشّ لميقات الجهاد فؤادُه فلا يتطرّقه البنان المخضّب
إذا الحرب قامت قام حتّى يعيدها قعودًا وحثحوثُ الكتيبة مُطنب
له كلَّ عامٍ غزوةٌ بمسوّم يقود المنايا رايُه حين يذهب
لُهام كأنّ البيض فى حجراته نجومُ سماءٍ نورها متجوّب
كراديس خيل لا تزال مغيرة بها المَلِك الرومىّ عانٍ معذّب
كأنّ بنات اليون بعد إيابه موزّعةً بين الصحائب ربرب
مواهبُ مغبوطٌ بها من ينالها صفايا سبايا الروم بكر وثيّب
وما قصدتْ قوما مُحِلّين خيلُه فتصرف إلّا عن دماءٍ تَصَبَّب
جدير بترك النائبات إذا غدا لهنّ على القتلى عويل ومندب
أغرّ هشامىّ القناةِ إذا انتمَى نَمَتْه بُدورٌ ليس فيهنّ كوكب
جميل المحيّا حين راح كأنّما تُخُيِّرَ فى ديباجة الوصف مُذهَب
يزين سرير الملك زينًا ويبتهى به المنبرُ المنصوبِ فى يوم يخطب

(٣٦)

مالكىّ تنشقّ عن وجهه الحرب كما انشقّت الدجا عن ضياء
أيّها السائلى عن الحزم والنجدة والبأس والندى والوفاء
إنّ تلك الخلال عند ابن سلم ومزيدًا من مثلها فى الغَناء
كخراج السماء سيبُ يديه لقريب ونازح الدارِ ناء
حرّم الله أن ترى كابن سلم عقبة الخير مُطعم الفقراء
يسقط الطيرُ حيث ينتثر الحَبّ وتُغشَى منازلُ الكرماء
ليس يعطيك للرجاء ولا الخوف ولكن يلذّ طعمَ العطاء
إنّما لذّة الجوادِ ابنِ سلم فى عطاءٍ ومركب للقاء
لا يهاب الوغى ولا يعبد المال ولكن يُهينه للثناء
أريحىّ له يد تمطر النيل وأخرى سمّ على الأعداء
قد كسانى خزًا وأخدمنى الحور وحلّى بنيّتى فى الجلاء
وحبانى به أغرّ طويل الباع صلْت الخدّين غضّ الفتاء
فقضى الله أن يموت كما مات بَنونا وسالفُ الآباء
راح فى نعشه ورُحْتُ الى عقبة أشكو فقال غير نِجاء
إن يكن منصف أُصيبَ فعندى عاجلٌ مثلُه من الوصفاء

فتنجزتُه أشمّ كجَرْوِ الـليث غاداك خارجا من ضراء
فجزى الله عن أخيك ابنَ سلم   حين قلّ المعروف خيرَ جزاء
صنعتنى يداه حتّى كأنّى   ذو ثراء من سِرّ أهل الثراء
لا أبالى صفح اللئيم ولا تجـ   ـرى دموعى على الخؤون الصفاء
يشترى الحمد بالثنا ويرى الذ   مّ فظيعا كالحيّة الرقشاء
ملك يفرع المنابر بالفضـ   ـل ويسقى الدماء يوم الدماء
كم له من يد علينا وفينا   وأيادٍ بيض على الأكفاء
أسدٌ يقضم الرجالَ وإن شئـ   ـت فغيثٌ أجشُّ ثرُّ السماء
قائم باللواء يدفع بالمو   ت رجالا عن حرمة الخلفاء
فعلى عقبة السلام مقيما   وإذا سار تحت ظلّ اللواء

(٣٧)

أمسى سليمان مرؤوما نطيف به   كما تطيف ببيت القبلة العرب
ترى عليه جلالا من أبوّته   ونصرةً من يد تندى وتنتهب
يبدو لك الخير فيه حين تنظره   كما بدا فى ثنايا الكاعب الشنب
عالى سليمانَ فى علياءَ مشرفةٍ   سيفٌ ورمحٌ وآباءٌ له نُجُب
يا نِعْمَ من كان منهم فى محلّته   وكان يشرب بالماء الذى شربوا
كانوا ،ولا دينَ إلّا السيف، مُلكهمُ   راسٍ وأيّامهم عاديّة غُلُب
تطول أعمارُ قومٍ فى أكفّهمِ   حينًا وتقصر أحيانا إذا غضبوا
العاقدين المنايا فى مسوّمة   يُزجِى أوائلَها الإيجافُ والخبب
بيضٌ جِدادٌ وأشراف زبانية   يغدو على من يعادى الويلُ والحرب
أقول للمشتكى دهرا أضرّ به   فيه ابتذال وفى أنيابه شعب
لا جار إلّا سليمان وأسرته   من العدوّ ومن دهر به نكب
إذا لقيتَ أبا أيّوب فى قَعَد   أو غازيا فوقه الرايات تضطرب
لاقيتَ دُفّاع بحرٍ لا يضعضعه   للمشرعين على أرجائه شرب
فاشربْ هنيئًا وذيّلْ فى صنائعه   وانعم فإنّ قعود الناعم اللعب
الهاشمىّ ابن داود تداركنا   وما لنا عنده نُعمَى ولا نسب
أحيا لنا العيشَ حتّى اهتزّ ناضرُه
وجارَنا فانجلت عنّا به الكرب
ليث لدى الحرب يُذكيها ويُخمِدها
ولا ترى مثل ما يعطى وما يهب
صعبًا مرارا وتاراتٍ نوافقه   سهلا عليه رواق المُلك واللجب

ساقى الحجيج أبوه الخير قد علمتْ   عُليا قريشٍ له الغايات والقصب
وافى حُنينا بأسيافه ومقربة   شعبِ النواصى بَراها القود والخبب
يعطى العداعن رسول الله مهجته   حتّى ارتدى زينها والسيف مختضب
وكان داود طودًا يُستظلّ به   وفى علىّ لأعداء الهدى هرب
والفضل عند ابن عبّاس تُعَدّ له   فى دعوة الدين آثارٌ ومحتسب
قل للمباهى سليمانَ وأسرتَه   هيهات ليس كعود النبعة الغرب
رَشِّحْ أباك لأخرى من صنائعه   واعرف لقوم برأس دونه أشب
أبناء أملاكٍ من صلّى لقبلتنا   فكلّهم مَلِكٌ بالتاج معتصب
دمُ النبىّ مشوب فى دمائهم   كما يخالط ماء المزنة الضرب
لو ملّك الشمسَ قومٌ قبلهم ملكوا   شمس النهار وبدر الليل لا كذب
أعطاهم الله ما لم يعط غيرهم   فهم ملوك لأعداء النُهى رُكُب
لا يحدبون على مال بمبخلة   إذا اللئام على أموالهم حدبوا
لولا فضولُ سليمان ونائلُه   لم يَدْرِ طالب عرف أين ينشعب
ينتابه الأقرب الساعى بذمّته   إذا الزمان كبا، والخابط الجنب
كم من يتيم ضعيف الطَرْف ليس له
إلّا تناول كفَّىْ ذى الغنى أشب
آخى له عروةَ الأَثْرَى فنال بها   رواحَ آخرَ معقودٍ له سبب
بنائل سبط لا مَنّ يردفه   إذا معاشر منّوا الفضل واحتسبوا
يا ابن الأكارم آباءً ومأثرةً   منك الوفاء ومنك النائل الرغب
فى الحىّ لى دَرْدَقٌ شعث شقيت بهم
لا يكسبون وما عندى لهم نشب
عزّ المضاغ عليهم بعد وجبتهم   فما ترى فى أُناس عيشهم وجب ؟